The Altered Object

Techniques, Projects, Inspiration

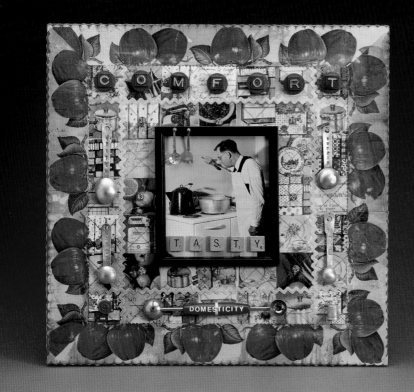

Terry Taylor

LARK BOOKS

A Division of Sterling Publishing Co., Inc.
New York

Library of Congress Cataloging-in-Publication Data

Taylor, Terry, 1952-
    The altered object : techniques, projects, inspiration / Terry Taylor. —
1st ed.
        p.   cm.
    Includes index.
    ISBN 1-57990-879-9 (hardcover)
    1. Handicraft.   I. Title.
    TT857.T4 2006
    745.5—dc22

                                    2006015572

10 9 8 7 6 5 4 3 2 1

First Edition

Published by Lark Books, A Division of Sterling Publishing Co., Inc.
387 Park Avenue South, New York, N.Y. 10016

Text © 2006, Lark Books
Photography © 2006, Lark Books, unless otherwise specified

Front cover: Michael de Meng, *Eye Above, River Below*

Distributed in Canada by Sterling Publishing, c/o Canadian Manda Group,
165 Dufferin Street, Toronto, Ontario, Canada M6K 3H6

Distributed in the United Kingdom by GMC Distribution Services,
Castle Place, 166 High Street, Lewes, East Sussex, England BN7 1XU

Distributed in Australia by Capricorn Link (Australia) Pty Ltd.,
P.O. Box 704, Windsor, NSW 2756 Australia

If you have questions or comments about this book, please contact:
Lark Books
67 Broadway
Asheville, NC 28801
(828) 253-0467

Manufactured in China

ISBN 13: 978-1-57990-879-9
ISBN 10: 1-57990-879-9

For information about custom editions, special sales, premium and corporate
purchases, please contact Sterling Special Sales Department at 800-805-5489
or specialsales@sterlingpub.com

Art Director: Kathleen Holmes
Cover Designer: Barbara Zaretsky
Assistant Editor: Nathalie Mornu
Associate Art Director: Shannon Yokeley
Art Production Assistant: Jeff Hamilton
Editorial Assistance: Delores Gosnell
Photographer: Martin Fox Photography
        (Martin Fox and Sallye Fox)

Contents

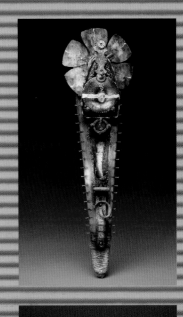

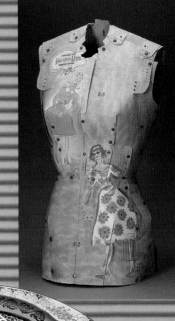

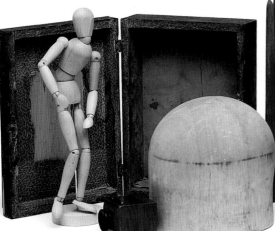

Introduction

WHAT IS AN ALTERED OBJECT? Could it be a wooden mannequin head with objects attached to it? The bleached carapace of a turtle with a hidden secret treasure? Is it a pair of rusted scissors mounted on a cutting board? If your answer is "yes" to these questions, you already know what an altered object is. If you aren't sure, let me explain.

An altered object is a two- or three-dimensional object that has been transformed into a work of art through the use of both traditional and non-conventional art techniques. The object can serve as a unique canvas for artistic expression. This approach alters preconceived notions about an object by challenging a viewer's conventional way of looking at and thinking about it. An altered object engages the viewer in a contemplative dialogue with it—and, by extension, with the artist who created the piece.

Creating an altered object doesn't require you to use fine art skills, such as drawing, painting, or sculpting. However, if you have those skills, by all means use them! Altering makes use of both two- and three-dimensional objects as surfaces and as working materials. It calls on elements of collage and assemblage, as well as simple-to-master crafting techniques. This range of materials and approaches is one of the reasons this form of artistic expression appeals to a wide variety of people.

As you read this book and look at more than 20 projects by 14 different artists, please, resist the temptation to recreate a particular object exactly. The projects are here to inspire you. In this book instructions are more an examination of process; they aren't step-by-step directions. You won't find precise measurements, colors of paint to use, or where to purchase identical objects.

I urge you to read the artists' comments before you look at the materials and process descriptions for their pieces. These comments reveal something valuable about how or why the artist was inspired to create a particular piece. Sometimes a unique object was the inspiration; at other times, an anonymous photograph, an

Above: **Terry Taylor**
Lesson Learned, 2004
9 x 7 inches (22.9 x 17.8 cm);
scissors 3¼ x 2½ inches (8.3 x 6.4 cm)
Antique metal frame, board, graphite paint, chalk, vintage scissors, milagro, sterling silver, sterling silver rivets, rusted nails
Collection of Brigid Burns and Chris Kobler
Photo © Steve Mann

event, or even a response to a theme served as the artist's springboard.

Once you've read an artist's comments, look at the specific object. What experience of your own could you bring to a similar object? Using memories or bits of random information, and creating or reinterpreting stories can be the catalysts for your own work.

If you find yourself thinking, "I can't possibly do anything like that," let me urge you to try. And don't sell short the skills you already possess. My bet is that you have a few tricks in your repertoire that some of these artists don't. If an artist used a unique method to create a project in this book or had a helpful hint to offer about a specific technique, you'll learn about both and can use them in one of your own creations. That's the best thing about reading books like this one: We can learn from other people's experience.

You'll also find within these pages an intriguing gallery of works by 10 featured artists, each of whose style and approach to altering objects is different. I chose them because their work speaks to me; I admire what they create. They use a variety of objects to suggest different ways of looking at the world, to evoke particular emotions, or to question our perceptions and preconceived notions.

I created a questionnaire for the artists to answer, so that we—both you and I—might learn something about what inspires them and about the processes they use. Where did they grow up? Which artists do they admire? Do their finished pieces end up looking the way they'd originally envisioned them? Why are they drawn to working with objects? Has their work changed over time?

Use this book as a guide for beginning your own journey with altered objects; let the works shown in it inspire you as you travel along your own road of creation. Select an object to alter because it has specific associations for you. When you combine it with carefully chosen imagery, text, or other objects, you're bound to elicit a thoughtful response from a viewer.

By identifying your own vision—what you wish to say—and expressing it in your art pieces, you'll join the ranks of artists who revel in their own unique creativity.

Above left: **Terry Taylor**
Mi Padre, Mi Madre, 2004
Each pendant, 2¾ x 1¼ inches (5.9 x 3.1 cm)
Found chain, fishing bobbers, sterling silver, milagros, miniature padlock

Above right: **Terry Taylor**
Cut, 2005
10 x 4½ x 2½ inches (25.4 x 11.4 x 6.4 cm)
Wood, found scissors, cock spurs, vintage pinback, rusted can lid, sterling silver, image transfer

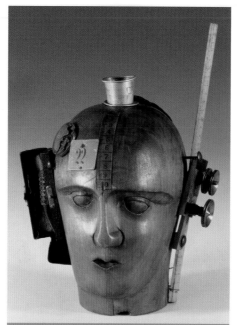

Raoul Hausmann
The Spirit of Our Times (Mechanical Head), 1919
12¾ x 8¼ x 7⅞ inches (32.5 x 21 x 20 cm)
Wooden head with various attached objects
© ARS, NY. CNAC/MNAM/Dist. Réunion des Musées
Nationaux /Musee National d'Art Moderne, Centre Georges
Pompidou, Paris, France. Art Resource, NY

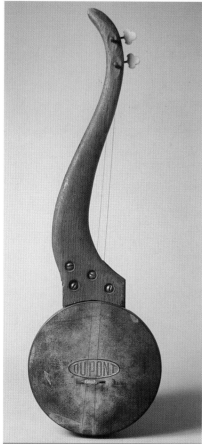

Bobby Hansson
The Dupont Baby Sitar, circa 1967
19 x 7 x 2½ inches (48.3 x 17.8 x 6.4 cm)
Film canister, mirror holder salvaged from
dresser, tuning peg, banjo string
Photo © artist
Collection of Wustum Museum, Racine, WI

Huɴᴀɴ ʙᴇɪɴɢs ʜᴀᴠᴇ ʙᴇᴇɴ altering objects for centuries. In early cultures, ritual objects and objects of adornment were embellished with feathers, small bones, shells, and other natural objects. Larger natural objects—skulls, skins, shells, and antlers—served as bases for embellishment. The natural objects were transformed from their natural state (altered, if you will) by the hand of man.

In the spirit of re-use and make-do, "country folk" of many nations fashioned utilitarian (and sometimes decorative) objects by using parts of other objects. Bobby Hansson's *The Dupont Baby Sitar* (circa 1967) reflects that spirit. A wholly unexpected version of a musical instrument is fashioned out of a piece of furniture, a film canister (the Dupont fortune is built on the manufacturing of film for various uses), tuning pegs, and banjo strings.

When looking at the broad variety of contemporary assemblage art—or altered objects, to use that term—it's evident that things haven't changed much over the centuries. Creative makers use found objects as embellishments, or change the intended uses for or meanings of those objects, to fashion wholly new altered objects.

Collage and assemblage—the very foundations of altered art—were begrudgingly recognized and only reluctantly accepted as art techniques during the early part of the 20th century. Paintbrushes, oil paints, and canvases were a major source of expense for struggling artists, such as Pablo Picasso (1881–1973), Georges Braque (1882–1963), and Kurt Schwitters (1887–1948). Paper ephemera and junk were free for the taking. Collage—the pasting of two-dimensional articles onto a surface—gave their new paintings additional layers of meaning and metaphor. In turn, the use of these new elements expanded our perceptions and understandings of how art could be created without traditional "art" techniques. But it wasn't until 1961, when William C. Seitz curated a landmark show, *The Art of Assemblage*, at the Museum of Modern Art in New York City, that collage and assemblage received full attention. The show and its eye-opening (for the times) black-and-white illustrated catalog gave critical credence to works of art that were primarily assembled or made up of things not intended as art materials, rather than to art that was painted or drawn.

Around the same time that Picasso and Braque were using collage elements in their work, Raoul Hausmann (1886–1971) and Marcel Duchamp began to use three-dimensional objects in their sculptural work. Objects embellished with smaller objects, or unique found objects (a bottle rack or a urinal), stripped of their utilitarian references were used to create sculptures. Rather than wielding the traditional skills of carving, modeling, or casting, other artists began exploring how to use found objects to create sculptures.

Hausmann's 1919 sculpture *The Spirit of Our Times (Mechanical Head)* is an early example. Disparate objects—a crocodile wallet, a ruler, a collapsible cup, and camera parts—are attached to a hairdresser's wig-making dummy. Is this Hausmann's response to his vision of the overloaded transmissions of sound and information in the new century? Joseph Cornell (1903–1972), another pioneer in assemblage, enclosed delicate found objects from earlier centuries in the haunting environments of his handmade boxes.

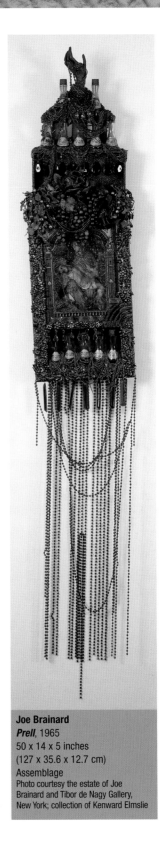

Joseph Cornell
Soap Bubble Set, 1936
15¾ x 14¼ inches (40 x 36.2 cm)
Glass case, insects
Photo © Wadsworth Atheneum Museum of Art, Hartford, CT. Purchased through the gift of Henry and Walter Keney. Art © The Robert and Joseph Cornell Memorial Foundation/Licensed by VAGA, New York, NY

In most of the art movements of the 20th century—surrealism, Dada, pop art, junk art, Fluxus, Arte Povera, and postmodernism—artists have used elements of collage and assemblage to create their work. Picasso, Duchamp, and Rauschenberg are well-known artists who have used assemblage in their work, and there are many more less immediately recognized artists as well.

For instance, Joe Brainard (1942–1994) may be better known for his collages and paintings, but he created many ornate assemblages with found objects during the heyday of the pop art movement. In *Prell* (1965), Joe lavishly embellished a constructed shrine with plastic grapes, beads, and bottles in shades of green and blue. The title alludes to a popular shampoo of the mid-1960s. Joe was undoubtedly influenced by television commercials for the product, which featured a solitary pearl floating languidly through a sea of green. When I first saw this piece in a retrospective show, I was entranced with its over-the-top baroque sensibility, its tresses of beads, and its fillip of a pop-culture title.

Joe Brainard
Prell, 1965
50 x 14 x 5 inches
(127 x 35.6 x 12.7 cm)
Assemblage
Photo courtesy the estate of Joe Brainard and Tibor de Nagy Gallery, New York; collection of Kenward Elmslie

In his sculpture *Nesso*, Giulio Paolini (1940-) reinterprets a bloody event in the mythic legend of Heracles—the slaying of a centaur who abducted his wife Deianira. With three simple elements—a plaster cast, a flowing length of silk, and an image of Heracles on paper—Paolini has created a shorthand, postmodern reference to the myth that captures the elegance of classical sculpture, while demonstrating a modern sensibility.

Sunnyland (On the Dark Side) by Betye Saar (1926-) combines images and objects that comment on issues of race and gender. The washboard serves as a canvas for a somber image that echoes the title of one of Billie Holliday's most famous songs. The striking image of the washerwoman comes from a

Betye Saar
Sunnyland (On the Dark Side), 1998
33½ x 16 x 2½ inches (85.1 x 40.6 x 6.4 cm)
Mixed media on vintage washboard; signed
Photo courtesy of Michael Rosenfeld Gallery, LLC, New York, NY

handcrafted whirligig. The choice of imagery and combination of objects create a powerfully moving piece.

Artists of all levels, from the professional exhibitor in international venues to the amateur working for sheer, personal pleasure, are now free to combine elements of collage and assemblage with other art or craft techniques. These methods are as acceptable as using a palette knife to layer oil paint on a canvas, or sculpting marble with a chisel and hammer. In this age of instantaneous visual information, it's impossible to escape the influence, if not the imagery itself, of artists who have created work in prior centuries, or the work of our contemporaries.

We're lucky to be able to look at the work of contemporary artists who post their work online or are published in books. (Can you imagine how art might have developed during the Renaissance if all of the artists had instant access to the art of their peers in other countries?) Let's embrace this gift of looking at the work of others, while striving to find our own voices and our own unique visual vocabularies of color, form, and imagery.

Giulio Paolini
Nesso, 1977
Height, 76¾ inches (195 cm)
Paper, silk, plaster
Photo © Stedelijk Museum, Amsterdam, Netherlands

The Basics

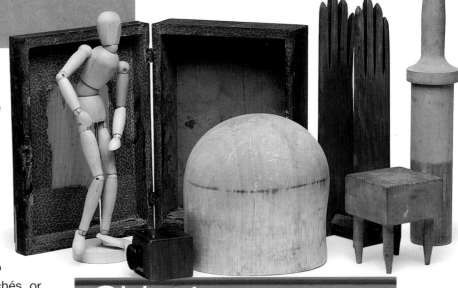

Which comes first, the object or the theme? It's like that age-old poultry conundrum, and there are no hard-and-fast answers. No one can tell you for sure that it's this way or the other. You simply have to discover your own working method.

Working with found objects—a photograph or a pile of tin cans—will lead you on an interesting adventure, but how will you get started? First, you must look at the object. Not a cursory glance: Really look at it, but not as something to be embellished with wings, pasted over with clichés, or covered with an assortment of dewy-eyed images.

Look at the object as if you were seeing at it for the first time. What story does it tell you? Does it remind you of an event, a specific time in history or in your life, a place, or a state of mind? How can you bring that story to life? If nothing comes immediately to mind, my advice is to put the object aside. It won't coalesce into a work of art no matter how you try to force it. But that doesn't mean you should stop thinking about it. After a while— perhaps an hour or years—you'll look at the object and something will click. I promise, it will click. You'll have an idea, and then the physical work can begin.

Creating an altered object can include these three primary elements: an object, imagery, and/or text. You can use any or all of the techniques and materials with which you're familiar from the worlds of fine art and general crafting, combining two or three elements to create a thought-provoking work that celebrates creativity and the human imagination.

My work evolves in two ways. It either starts with a theme that leads me to certain objects, or with objects that lead me to a certain theme.
—Michael de Meng

Objects

What can you alter? The question you really need to ask yourself is what can't I alter? If you can find a method to change the object with imagery or text, any object is fair game. Of course, I wouldn't recommend that you run to an antique store and purchase that genuine Louis-the-something-or-other fauteuil that you spotted in the window. At least not unless it's a real bargain. So, how do you select an object? At the risk of sounding mystical, objects speak to the artist in some manner— through their shapes, textures, or materials, or by association. For instance, tea towels are more than simple lengths of printed linen or colorful cotton, used to wipe up spills and dry dishes. They also adorn the kitchen. Sometimes they're displayed like art, simply because of their beauty. Look at objects you might pass by with fresh eyes—a fencing mask, a bird cage, or a rusted saw. What do they bring to mind? What do they tell you about themselves? By altering objects, we can create new meanings and associations for them.

To alter Sir Walter Scott's famous question, breathes there the man (or woman) with soul so dead, who never to him(her)self said: I want things!

Human beings seem to be—for better or worse—acquisitive creatures. We surround ourselves with objects, by accident or on purpose. Look around your

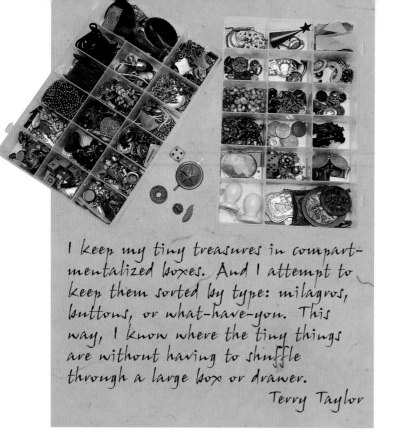

I keep my tiny treasures in compartmentalized boxes. And I attempt to keep them sorted by type: milagros, buttons, or what-have-you. This way, I know where the tiny things are without having to shuffle through a large box or drawer.

Terry Taylor

own living or work space. You'll see things you've held on to, even though they serve no function. Why? Because they speak to you.

I think that people who create altered objects or want to do so are inexplicably drawn to objects. We purchase them impulsively, or avidly seek them out. We may or may know exactly what to do with an object that we've purchased, but that doesn't matter. Meanwhile, we enjoy looking at it and thinking about what we can do to or with it. An object may sit on the shelf for longer than we care to admit, until one day, inspiration hits us.

Objects can be altered or used as materials for altering. Whether you purchase them in a craft or antique store, find them on the street, or have them stashed in the garage, you'll amass small objects of all shapes, sizes, and materials as you work. If you're drawn to assemblage and altered objects, you've probably got enough materials to work with. It goes with the territory. You know what materials and embellishments you've stored. Don't discount any of them. They can all be used. Maybe not right away, but someday (believe me) you'll want one specific thing and you'll be glad you saved it.

Attaching One Object to Another

The object or objects that you've chosen to work on dictate the methods you'll use to attach things. This may be obvious to you, but there's no harm in mentioning that you might not want to plan on embroidering or stitching on a piece of metal or using a screw to attach something to a piece of china. But, that doesn't mean that you can't sew on metal or use screws with china if that's the effect you'd like to achieve. Where there's a will, there's always a creative way.

Using Glue

Glues provide a quick and simple method of attaching almost anything to a surface. They're the workhorses used by almost all of the artists in this book. Every artist has his or her favorite glues. For a brief overview of glues, see page 17.

Using Hardware

When you think of wood surfaces, what immediately comes to mind? If you think of nails, you've hit the answer right on the head. Add screws, brads, staples, thumbtacks, and anything else that has a sharp, pointed end. For metal, you may want to use screws and bolts of different shapes and sizes. Consider investing in a

simple pop-rivet tool for joining two pieces of metal together. These tools are easy to use and inexpensive.

Here's a hint: Abandon your local craft store and prowl the aisles of your local home center or hardware store. Don't be afraid to ask the salespeople questions. More often than not, salespeople are fonts of information. If you can tell them which two items you might want to join, my bet is that they can give you two or three alternative ways to do it.

Joining with Heat

If you're bound and determined to work with metal, after you've exhausted all of the cold connections for joining metal (i.e., methods that don't require using heat), you'll want to explore soldering and welding. Joining with heat can be as simple as using a household soldering iron and lead solder, or as complex as arc welding.

Stitching

More and more artists are altering fabric objects these days. Unless you plan to invest in and use a very expensive, computerized, state-of-the-art sewing machine, nothing beats the simple pairing of a needle and thread. Sometimes, simple stitching is all that is needed.

Don't limit your stitching to fibers: try using wire in lieu of thread to attach metal to metal, or metal to another surface. And who's to say you can't drill holes in two pieces of wood and stitch the two together with bamboo yarn? Believe me, it's possible!

Imagery

Adding imagery to the surface of an object is a popular alteration method, whether you use a single image or a multitude of them. Images readily communicate to the viewer what you're trying to express. Whether these images are original or appropriated, however, they must work toward some purpose or meaning, or they become mere decorations. Creating and choosing imagery is an important step in the creative process, but don't fret about making choices. If an image has real meaning for you, that will be evident when someone other than yourself looks at the completed altered object.

Creating Your Own Imagery

Don't fret about your artistic abilities if you wish to create your imagery. You don't have to be a Norman Rockwell or Andrew Wyeth; each of us is capable of drawing, even if we're uncomfortable with the end results. It doesn't matter if we think the drawing is awful (we've all felt that way); even an awkward stick figure penciled onto an object will speak to the viewer.

Using personal imagery is another approach. Those stacks of out-of-focus or off-kilter snapshots, vintage family photographs, and even school pictures can all be effective. Grab your digital camera and create the images you think you need for a piece: an oak tree down the road, a sunset-streaked sky, or a speeding car. You don't have to be as skilled a photographer as Ansel Adams, if they serve your purpose, that's all that matters.

Other Sources of Imagery

If you choose not to create your own original images, be thankful that we live in a world awash in visual imagery. It's all around us: in junk mail and catalogs, abandoned snapshots found in antique stores, out-of-print books, and yesterday's newspaper.

I have a fat three-ring binder, filled to overflowing with images for use in my own work: Anatomy illustrations (hands and heads, especially), images of saints, and instructional photos from old Red Cross water-safety and first-aid manuals. Not to mention ten boxes filled with vintage and not-so-vintage postcards. As you work, you'll find different types and styles of imagery that appeal to you. When you find something that you like, file it away; you'll find yourself coming back to it again and again.

What's most important, I think, is choosing the imagery. First and foremost, the imagery must speak to you. If it doesn't, it won't elicit the response you intend from your viewer. For instance, don't use just any image of a house. Be deliberate and single-minded in your pursuit of the perfect image. A brick split-level sitting on a manicured expanse of lawn and an ivy-covered Victorian gingerbread cottage draw forth very different responses. A scrawled, childlike, stick drawing and an architectural blueprint can both portray the same house, but from different points of view.

I like to purchase old, out-of-print books, magazines, and art catalogs in secondhand shops and antique stores. Be forewarned that if you're not careful, your shelves will begin to sag.

For years I kept a 12-volume set of *Lives of the Saints* and learned the hard way that attempting to save whole books (or sets of books) for imagery takes up valuable shelf space.

Don't feel guilty about stripping books that you purchase for their images. And don't feel ashamed about using some of the original imagery from books (the actual pages!) in a piece that you're working on. Sometimes, it's just the right thing to do.

Your sources for imagery are boundless. Here's the real question: Is it okay to use imagery that you clipped from a magazine, found online, or discovered in an out-of-print book? Like all of life's crucial questions, the answer is both "no" and "yes."

As you know, copyright is the legal right granted to an artist to exclusive use (including sale, publication, or distribution) of his or her creative work. In other words, as the creator, I can do whatever I want with the work I've created. Frankly, none of us would be happy if others took credit for or profited from our creative work, especially without our knowledge or permission. If the spectre of copyright infringement concerns you, seek the advice of a law firm that specializes in copyright law. You'll get an answer to your specific questions from them. In addition, there are books on copyright law to read and a limitless selection of online sources to consult to inform your own decisions. Here's my personal opinion, speaking as an artist who uses imagery that is not my own: I don't claim to have created those images, and this fact is usually self-evident to anyone looking at my work. I am making a singular object and not an object for reproduction. I may use an historic image as a starting point for a piece, or use a portion of an image in the same way that a writer might quote another writer to illustrate an idea or strengthen an argument. Artists of all stripes have been doing just that for years. That said, just how does one transfer an image to an object?

Image Transfer Processes

Adding images to a surface is probably the most daunting aspect of creating altered art. Just how did the artist get that image onto that irregular surface? Where there's a will, there's a way. Chances are you already have a preferred method that you've used in other crafting projects.

There are two basic questions you need to ask yourself once you've selected an image to transfer: What surface am I working on? Is it wood, paper, metal, plastic, or fiber? And how do I want the finished image to look? Do I want an opaque image that sits on the surface, or a transparent image that allows the original surface or background elements to appear through it? Once you've answer these questions, you're ready to choose a process.

Collage

Collage is the simplest method for transferring imagery. You can transfer the original images or, better yet, color photocopies of the images you've selected. Collaged images are opaque. If you want a transparent or translucent image, you'll need to use a different type of transfer technique. Paper, wood, fiber, and even glass are suitable surfaces for collage.

> In the past I used real tintypes in my work; however, because of their unique history and their fragile nature, I decided to photocopy them and add pieces of mica on top in order to replicate the look of the actual photos and provide the photocopies with protective covers.
>
> —Jane Wynn

Rubber Stamping

With the appropriate ink, you can use rubber stamps on any surface. Layer stamped images atop one another, mask portions of the image, or use embossing pigments for dimensional effects. Pigment inks, dye-based inks, and solvent-based inks are available in a wide palette of colors. Each ink type has its specific use; the manufacturers' recommendations are printed on the packaging.

If you can't find a rubber stamp that you like, choose an image that will suit your needs and take it to a rubber-stamp manufacturer (usually your local sign shop). For a nominal cost, the manufacturer will make a custom-sized stamp for you.

Solvent Transfers

Black-and-white photocopies and clay-based (slick) magazine pages can be transferred to absorbent surfaces (paper, wood, and fabric) by using the solvent-transfer technique. The solvent breaks down the toners and inks on the paper and transfers the image to the surface. This technique is not foolproof; results vary depending on the image and solvents used. The transferred image is transparent and has a soft, painted appearance.

There are a number of different solvents. Some—acetone, toluene-based markers, and lighter fluid—require adequate ventilation when you use them. Nontoxic solvents include oil of wintergreen and citrus-based solvents.

The transfer process is straightforward. Lay your image facedown on the surface to which you want to transfer it, and lightly coat the image's reverse surface with the solvent of your choice. Burnish or rub the paper with a bone folder, spoon, or similar tool. As you work, periodically lift a corner of the image to check on the transfer progress.

Heat-Transfer Papers

These specially coated papers allow you to transfer an image that you've printed on them to another surface by using heat. Most copy shops will make heat transfers for you. You can also find heat-transfer papers for your home or office ink-jet printer. Heat transfers are applied facedown and ironed onto your surface. Keep in mind that you'll need to create a mirror-image copy if your image has text on it or if you want your image to be oriented in a particular direction. Heat transfers are best suited for fabric but can be used on paper as well. The image is opaque and sits on the surface.

Water-Slide Decals

Purchase commercially printed decals or create your own by using water-slide transfer paper. Water-slide decals are versatile, transparent image transfers that you can use on almost any type of surface, from glass to silk. You can purchase transfer paper for use with ink-jet printers and most types of toner-based photocopiers. For best results, follow the manufacturer's instructions carefully.

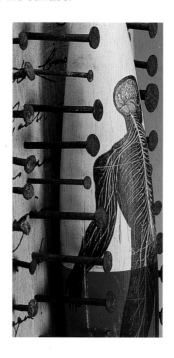

Acrylic-Medium Transfers

This transfer method is versatile. Apply acrylic mediums to photocopied images, using the technique described in this section. These transfers are translucent and sit on top of the surface to which they're applied. They work well on surfaces with irregularities and on curved surfaces, and they wrap around corners, too.

Lay a black-and-white or color photocopy face-up on a piece of glass. Tape the image to the glass. Brush the image with successive coats of acrylic medium, letting each coat dry before applying the next. Anywhere from five to twelve coats may be applied. The more coats you apply, the thicker your transfer will be.

After the layers of medium are thoroughly dry, remove the taped image from the glass. Soak the coated image in water and peel off the paper backing. Then use your fingers or a sponge to roll the remaining layers of paper from the transfer. Don't rub too vigorously—the moist transfer will easily stretch or tear. Finally, allow the transfer to dry, and then apply it to any surface with acrylic medium.

Packing-Tape Transfers

Tape transfers provide a quick, low-tech, and solvent-free way to place an image on a surface. The end result is translucent, and looks and functions like a sticker.

Place a glossy magazine picture or photocopy facedown onto the sticky side of a strip of clear packing tape. Place the taped image on a hard surface, with the tape facing down, then burnish the back of the image vigorously with a bone folder or spoon. Finally, remove the paper backing: dab the back of the image with a damp sponge, allow the paper to absorb the water, then rub off the paper backing with your fingers.

(If you'd prefer a matte finish instead of the glossy finish of the packing tape, lightly sand the surface of the tape with fine-grade sandpaper.) Apply the transfer to your surface with an acrylic medium.

Text

Artists have been adding text to their works since the invention of written language. Text may be added to identify an image or to convey additional meaning. It can be easily read or obscured. As with imagery, it should be chosen with careful thought. Words that are used too often and without careful, thoughtful choice become meaningless and empty.

Sources of Text

There are many ways to generate the text that you wish to use in your altered objects. Create lists of words while you look at the object you intend to work on, consult collections of quotations, use personal journal entries, or clip phrases that appeal to you from the magazines and newspapers you read. I have an ever-growing collection of old dictionaries that I turn to for both imagery and text; they're inexpensive and disposable.

In days past, your teacher or librarian would have had you consult an encyclopedia for textual information. Aren't you glad that you live in a world where typing one or two words into an Internet search engine gives you a universe of words and text from which to choose? Even remotely relevant links may fire your imagination. Jean Moore discovered a wonderful line by Coleridge by simply typing the word "sleep" into a search engine; she used that line in her piece shown on page 80.

How to Add Text

The easiest way to add text to a piece is to write it yourself. This conveys a sense of immediacy and adds a human touch. However, many people feel about their handwriting the same way they feel about their ability to draw. Fear not! There are many alternative ways to add text.

Rubber-stamp alphabets are available in many styles and sizes. In addition, you can choose from stamps with foreign phrases, and words or phrases written in foreign scripts. Clippings from printed texts, transfer lettering, stickers, metal letters, and game pieces can all be used to add text to your pieces. Use metal stamps to emboss lettering into metal. If you have access to an old-fashioned typewriter, type your text. Typewritten text on paper feels entirely different from computer-generated text, even with the wide selection of computer fonts that your computer has in its memory.

You can use transfer techniques for text as well. Just remember that if you're using a transfer that is placed facedown (heat transfers, solvent transfers, and some water-slide transfers), your text will be reversed. Reversed text can be intriguing visually, but it may not provide the effect you're after. If it doesn't, use the mirror options on your photocopier when you create your text.

Materials and Tools

Coloring Materials

What are your favorites? Fluid inks, acrylic paints, markers, pencils, pastels, gouaches, encaustics, or stamping inks? You know what to expect with these. When new coloring materials appear on the market, purchase a few and experiment with them. If you like them, add them to your bag of coloring tricks and continue to use them. It's never a good idea to try new coloring materials (or techniques) on a project before you've tested them.

Use any type of coloring materials to alter objects. As long as the material is compatible with your surface, you can use it. Some surfaces—plastic, glass, and metal—may need special consideration. Follow your instincts and when in doubt, read the label on any new coloring material.

Papers and Fibers

Isn't it wonderful that we aren't restricted to the primary colors of our childhood construction paper? The large selection of papers now available can be overwhelming. I try (note that "try" is the operative word here) to keep mine sorted by type, placing handmade papers in one file and patterned papers in another.

Buying papers (or fabric or yarn) is a harmless addiction. Nevertheless, it's an addiction with which many of us struggle. Asian papers, corrugated papers, handmade papers with inclusions, translucent vellums, patterned papers for scrapbooking, and novelty papers that are flocked or gilded: I want them all, even when I don't have an immediate use for them.

Add bits of recycled papers (a more prosaic term for "ephemera") to your stash. Save those charming tea labels, foil wrappers, chopstick envelopes, cancelled stamps, postcards, advertisements, and strips from fortune cookies. They'll come in handy one day.

Scraps of silk, damaged quilts, lacy oddments, scraps of leather, and varieties of strings and threads can also be used for altering objects. A word to the wise: Try to save only those papers, fabrics, and threads that are truly unique and special. Otherwise, your workspace will be overrun.

Tools

Tools that you own for household maintenance, such as a hammer, small saw, pliers, wire cutters, a drill, and drill bits, may be useful for some projects. Use a heat gun (for removing paint) to speed up the paint-drying process or to activate embossing powders. If you don't have one, a hair dryer will work just as well. Handheld rotary tools may be used for drilling, cutting, abrading, and many other purposes. There's an attachment for you to use for any task you need to accomplish.

Cutting tools—scissors of all types and a craft knife—are essential tools. Keep a pair of everyday scissors on hand, as well as an assortment of decorative-edge scissors and a pair of small, sharp,

pointed scissors reserved solely for precision cutting. Be sure to keep a supply of sharp blades on hand for your craft knife: You'll achieve precise and smooth cuts with a sharp blade. If you're working with metal you'll need cutting tools just for metal, such as a jewelry saw or metal shears. Whatever you do, don't use a cutting tool on a material that it wasn't intended to cut. Even if the tool is handy and will work, use the correct tool for the job.

Keep brushes of all sizes and types near your worktable. There's nothing more pleasing to look at than a container chock-full of a variety of brushes. Use them for painting, stippling, varnishing, and gluing. As with all your tools, keep your brushes in good working condition by cleaning them thoroughly after you use them. Acrylic mediums and paints dry more quickly than you might think. Keep a container of water nearby for soaking your brushes until you can clean them.

Glues and Adhesives

The best advice anyone can offer about specific glue can be found on the label. When you shop for glue, keep two questions in mind. Are my surfaces porous or nonporous? Do I want a strong, long-lasting bond or a temporary one? Once you've answered these questions, you can determine whether or not the glue you're considering is right for the job.

White Glues

White glues are widely used for all types of craft applications and are readily available. These all-purpose glues are usually water soluble, clear drying, and somewhat flexible. You can use them on almost all surfaces, from paper to ceramics and fabric to some plastics. They're not recommended for use on metals or anything that will come in contact with water. Many—if not most—white glues are PVA (polyvinyl acetate adhesive) glues. Many different brands exist, with consistencies ranging from thin to thick. In general, these glues can be thinned with water as desired.

Acrylic Mediums

Acrylic mediums are made of polymer emulsions. When dry, they form durable, flexible, nonyellowing films. They serve to bind the pigments in acrylic paints. Mediums are available in different viscosities and sheens. In general, you can use acrylic mediums with paper and other porous surfaces, as you would most white glues.

Hot Glue

Hot glue bonds quickly and works well on both porous and nonporous surfaces. It works especially well for bonding uneven surfaces to each other. Don't use this glue for structural purposes (the bond is easily broken), and limit its use with paper projects.

Cyanoacrylate Glues

These are the wonder glues of the modern world. Adjectives such as "super" or "crazy" usually indicate that the glue is a cyanoacrylate variety. Just a drop (literally!) usually does the trick. They are quick-bonding, clear, and strong. Surfaces must fit tightly together in order for these glues to work well. Their power is wasted on paper crafts, and they may not work well with some plastics.

Industrial-Strength Adhesives

Two-part epoxies, jewelry glues, silicone glues, china glues, multipurpose cements, and contact adhesives all fall into this category. They all offer a strong bond for hard-to-glue materials, such as metals, ceramics, rubber, fiberglass, plastics, and glass. They are clear when dry and can sometimes be used as sealants. When you work with them, provide plenty of ventilation and follow the manufacturer's instructions carefully.

Spray Adhesives

These adhesives are great for covering large, flat surfaces, such as papers and fabrics. Use them in well-ventilated areas and cover your work area to protect it from overspray. Objects sprayed with these adhesives can be repositioned. For a more permanent bond, coat both surfaces to be joined and allow them to become tacky or dry before joining them. Just follow the manufacturer's recommendations.

Wood Glues

Wood glues are generally divided into two types: AR (aliphatic resin) and polyurethane glues. AR adhesives are common yellow wood glues for interior use. Polyurethane glues are fine for both interior and exterior applications.

Glue Sticks

These glues are usually acid-free and specifically formulated for use on paper, cardboard, fabric, and photographs. Some are permanent; others permit repositioning. In general, they are clear drying and less susceptible to wrinkling than more fluid glues.

Five Tins, Five Ways

What is it about boxes that appeals to us as artists? Perhaps they remind us of the boxes we used as kids to stash our precious finds in—our rocks, feathers, rusty nails, and stamps. Or do they stir memories of birthday and holiday surprises? Why do Cornell's mysterious boxes appeal to us?

Although I can't answer these questions, I can say—with certainty—that boxes are wonderful stages or canvases, for assemblage and collage. They're inexpensive and easy to find, and what a variety there is to choose from: Craft boxes, matchboxes, antique boxes, and cigar boxes, to name just a few.

I thought it would be fun to ask four other artists to create an altered object using a ubiquitous metal candy tin. Unless you've been lost and living in the shifting sands of the Sahara, my bet is you know precisely which brand of tin I'm talking about. We all started out with a tin of

the same size and brand, but what we did with our tins is as distinct from one another as our differences as human beings.

Two artists created wholly original fantasies, two artists drew on personal experience, and one artist used a tin to express her sociopolitical feelings. We used paint, altered the surfaces of bare metal, placed three-dimensional objects inside the boxes, on top of the boxes, and—in one particularly intriguing example—cut a box apart, leaving only a vestige of its former shape and size.

Box Basics

It's easiest to work on lidded mint tins if the lid and body are separated. Use needle-nose pliers to carefully bend back each of the simple hinges that join the lid to the box. Bend them back only as far as is needed to slip the lid off the hinges. Once you've done that, you face two creative challenges. First, how do you change the surface of the box? And second, how do you attach elements placed inside or on the outside of the box?

Surface Treatments

Use any craft technique you can think of to transform a box's surface. Painting techniques and decoupage are quick and easy. Adhere paper or fabric to the surface of a box with acrylic mediums. Glue mosaic or mirror tiles to a box. The possibilities are endless.

Paint strippers will remove the bright paint on your tin, but choose your paint stripper wisely—some are more caustic than others. Be sure to read the manufacturer's directions for the particular stripper you're using. Cover your work surfaces, make sure there's adequate ventilation in your workspace, and wear protective gloves. Eye protection and breathing masks may be required as well.

Use a sanding sponge to abrade the paint. You can take off as much or as little as you

Change the color of the bare metal with any number of chemical solutions. Darken or tarnish the metal with oxidizing agents, such as liver of sulphur and or chemicals for blackening silver, brass, and copper. You'll find these oxidizing agents at most bead stores. You can create patinas—rust or verdigris—with chemical solutions purchased in craft stores. Read the manufacturer's instructions before using any of these solutions. Simply sanding the tins and adding some green patina solution makes for quick rust!

—Jane Wynn

wish. Sanding also gives bare metal a brushed look. You can refine the brushed look of metal even further with a household scouring pad. If you have a simple, handheld rotary tool, use an abrasive pad with it. This works much faster than hand sanding.

Adding Elements

This is the fun part and is sometimes a true test of one's ability to think on one's feet. There are no hard-and-fast rules for adding elements to boxes. They can be attached (or not) in various ways. Many of Joseph Cornell's boxes include moving objects (rings, balls, or papers) in combination with fixed objects (see page 7). You may wish to include moveable objects in your boxes.

Attaching elements to metal boxes can be achieved in three ways: gluing, soldering, or riveting. You can even seemingly suspend objects in air!

Gluing is the easiest method to use. Soldering is an option when working with metal, but it presents certain problems (heat will char painted metal surfaces) and skills that aren't used in the projects in this book. Choosing to use a cold connection, such as riveting or wiring, is a way to avoid marring painted metal. If your metal isn't painted and you have experience with a soldering iron or torch, then use those skills.

I rust metal objects the old-fashioned way when I don't have an immediate use for them. I leave the objects outdoors—hidden in the garden or on the back porch—for this treatment. To speed nature's progress, I abrade the metal with sandpaper, then fill a spray bottle with cider vinegar and mist the metal. Every few days or so, I spray the metal with the vinegar solution. Over time, the acidic vinegar, in combination with the open air, rusts the metal. It's not a quick and easy process, but I find it satisfying nonetheless.

—Terry Taylor

Riveting

Riveting elements to boxes with eyelets, brass nails, or even pop rivets is real metalwork. Metalworkers refer to these techniques as cold connections. You'll find many colors, shapes, and types of eyelets in craft stores, and brass nails and pop rivets in home-improvement or hardware stores. And they're really easy to use.

1 Mark the location where you want to place a rivet. Use an awl or a center punch to make a dimple in the metal.

2 Drill a hole the same size as your eyelet's stem or the diameter of a brass nail in both the box and the piece you wish to attach. If you're working with a brass nail, cut it slightly longer than the combined thickness of the box material and the material or object you wish to attach.

3 Hold the drilled pieces with the eyelet or nail inserted, and turn the assembly over. Use a hammer and setting tool to spread the stem of the eyelet. To set the end of your brass-nail rivet, carefully tap along the edge of the cut nail; you'll see that the metal moves out. Continue to tap until the metal nail is wider than the drilled hole.

Suspending Objects

Don't limit yourself to simply gluing objects to a box surface. You can float or suspend objects, too. It may take a little longer to accomplish, but the results are often very effective. Suspend objects with thread and wire, or build supports out of small bits of wood or foam-core board to push items out and away from the box.

When you drill your holes or set eyelets in a metal box, you'll find it useful to support the metal on a small block of wood that fits inside the box.

−Terry Taylor

la mano poderosa
(the powerful hand)

CREATED BY TERRY TAYLOR

Find inspiration in your favorite objects or imagery to create your own personal, portable shrine. It won't (and it shouldn't) look like anyone else's.

materials

Tin

Matte acrylic spray varnish

Photographs and loteria cards

Metal frontispiece

Washi paper

Matte acrylic medium

Vintage dictionary text

Foam-core board

Spray adhesive

Bronze charm

Brass nails

How-to Tip

I remove the paint from mint tins by tossing them in the fireplace every time I build a fire. (Somehow, this justifies lolling in front of a fire on a winter's eve as creative time.) When I retrieve the tins from the ashes, I use an abrasive kitchen scrub pad to even out the charred, flaky surfaces. And then, to preserve the dark color, I spray the surfaces with a light coat of matte varnish.

process

1 There are many ways to change the surface of your tin. Do you have a favorite? If not, then read the techniques on page 19 and try one that appeals to you.

2 I took my inspiration for this piece from the images and objects which I have arrayed above my computer in my office.

On driving trips, the sight of a fortune-teller's sign makes me swerve onto the shoulder or make a U-turn. I looked through my stored photographs and selected a few images. I photocopied and reduced them to fit inside the tin.

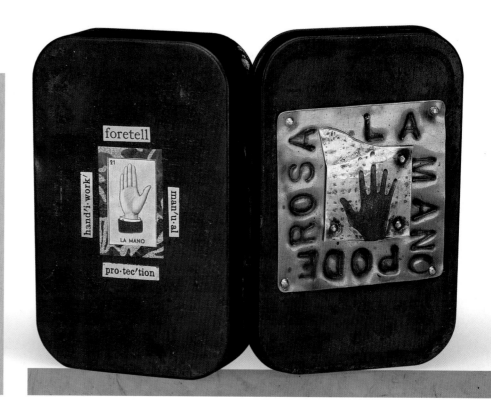

3 I created the brass and silver medallion on the front of the box in a metals class several years ago. Although I never considered it a finished work, I kept it to remind me of the class and a place in time. Once I decided that the piece shown here would feature hands, I looked for my metal work in the morass that is my studio at home (no small task!).

Brass nails were used as rivets to attach the medallion to the front lid of the box (see page 21).

4 Washi paper was applied to the interior of the tin with acrylic medium. In addition, I cut the place names where the photos were taken—Los Angeles and Santa Fe—from a vintage dictionary. I adhered the place names to the metal with acrylic medium.

5 The photocopies were mounted onto mat or foam-core board with spray adhesive.

A shrine to La Mano Poderosa—the powerful hand—both blesses and protects my office. It includes an uncarved, scout neckerchief slide kit, paintings, milagros, a cookie cutter, an X ray, and photos from my journeys. The hand is a powerful image for me: It's a symbol of protection, creation, and—sometimes—prognostication. I find myself using La Mano Poderosa again and again in different forms.

Terry Taylor

Mounting the photos—rather than gluing them directly to the tin—gives a sense of depth. On one of the photos, I glued a bronze charm that a friend had brought to me from her trip to India. To create a faux rivet, I cut a brass nail with snips, put a drop of glue on the cut end, and then pushed the nail into the board.

6 A loteria card photocopy was glued to the back of the tin

with matte medium. I selected "handy" words from a dictionary, cut them out, and adhered them to the tin as well.

Terry Taylor
La Mano Poderosa, 1999
12 x 6 x 2 inches (30 x 15 x 5 cm)
Tin reflector, tin tart pan, tin hand ornament
Photo © Evan Bracken
Collection of Patricia Arcuri

Terry Taylor
Mano, 2001
6¾ x 5¾ x 1½ inches (17 x 14.6 x 3.8 cm)
Metal frame, wood, ceramic hand, Red Cross pin, screening wire

the autumn of her years

CREATED BY ERIC ALLEN MONTGOMERY

Eric's elegiac tribute to his mother is a clear reminder to us all that the impetus of any work of art should come from within.

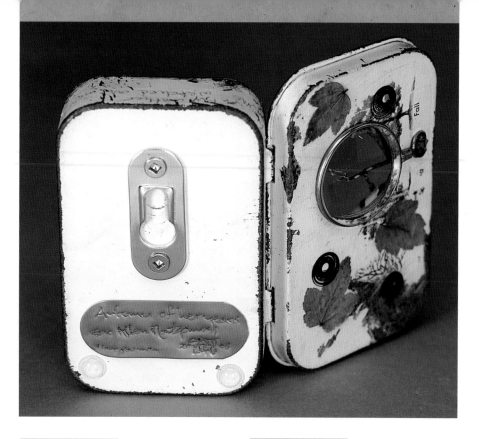

materials

Tin

Acrylic enamel spray paint

Vintage imagery

Waterslide transfer decal

Acrylic matte medium

Photographs

Leaves and twigs

Watch parts

Optician's lens holder

Magnifying lens

Keyhole hanger

Industrial-strength glue

Washi papers

Found wood

Photographs

Thin aluminum sheet

Leather

Thin plywood squares

Semiprecious stone heart

Copper foil

process

1   Eric stripped his tin to the bare metal and then repainted it with an acrylic enamel spray paint. He told me, "It seems completely pointless to have stripped the paint in the first place. But at least it feels like a clean slate and all mine."

2   Images of trees from a children's science book that belonged to his mother were copied to create a waterslide transfer decal. Eric applied the decal to the painted surface of the tin. After the decal dried, Eric gave the transferred imagery a light coat of matte medium. Then he cut out the circular opening with a jewelry saw.

3   Eric subtly distressed the painted tin surfaces with sandpaper, paying particular attention to the edges. He resealed the surfaces with a coat of acrylic matte medium. The sides of the tin were inscribed with pencil: "My mother watched over me. My mother is lost to me." A second coat of medium was added to protect the inscriptions. Eric applied tiny, dried leaves and watch springs to the lid with matte medium.

4   Not so very long ago, optician's lenses were hard to find, but now you can find reproductions in many craft stores. Eric removed the lens from a vintage optician's lens holder and replaced it with a magnifying lens. He glued the reassembled lens over the circular opening on the lid.

5   Before starting to work on the interior portions of the box, Eric attached a keyhole hanger to the back of the tin. Here's a lesson to learn: Always attach any hanging devices to your work early on in the process. Attaching hanging devices after all work is finished is just asking for heartbreak and trouble.

6   Washi paper was applied to the inner face of the lid with matte medium. Eric cut out an opening on a piece of recycled wood, matching the dimensions of the circular opening on the front of the lid. The wood was then glued to the lid.

7 Eric scanned a photograph of his mother as a young girl, printed it out, and then mounted the image on a thin sheet of aluminum. He used deckle-edged scissors to trim the image. The aluminum backing allowed Eric to curl the photo slightly, giving it dimension. Again, leaves and watch parts were adhered to the wood with acrylic medium. Finally, the photo was glued in place.

8 Using a wood-burning tool, Eric wrote additional text on a scrap of leather. He mounted the leather on thin plywood and glued it inside the box. Leaves and watch parts were glued to the leather. A second photograph of Eric's mother was scanned and mounted on a thin aluminum sheet. The photograph was cut out, backed with tiny squares of plywood to give it depth, and glued into place.

9 Eric added a small twig and a small, stone heart to the composition. To stiffen the leaves before attaching them to the twig, Eric painted their backs with several coats of acrylic matte medium.

10 It's a nice touch (and a point of pride in your work) to sign a finished piece. Eric used a ballpoint pen to emboss a piece of copper foil with the title of the piece, the date, and his signature. The copper foil was glued to the back of the tin.

I've been making what I call my Pocket Watchers for a few years now, converting mint tins and other metal tins into pocket-sized portable shrines. These are designed to commemorate people (real or imagined) who will watch over us like guardian angels, patron saints, or personal demons. I like the idea of making something that I can tuck in my pocket, place on a shelf, or hang over my bed, knowing that I am watched over and cared for, even if it's by a creature of my imagining or a public hero I'll never actually meet.

Autumn of Her Years is a memorial to my mother, Jane Montgomery. She was only 60 when the first symptoms of what was soon diagnosed as Alzheimer's began to affect her. When I made this tribute, a mere eight years later, she was still alive and well, but completely gone to my father, my siblings, and me. She will never again telephone to wish me a happy birthday, send me a postcard, or share a story, yet she is not dead.

This is my way of keeping her near me—the young girl I never knew (she is only four in the left-hand picture), following the floating feather of her dreams. I used the last good photo, which I took of my mom on New Year's Day, 2003, while she still looked at me with knowledge and love in her eyes. Months later she was gone, but she is with me in my memories and in my heart.

Eric Allen Montgomery

miss tibbit's trophy

CREATED BY JANE WYNN

Miss Hattie Pearl Tibbit—a spinsterish librarian—was born in Calhoun County, Arkansas, on February 12, 1880. She wore this pendant as she shushed intemperate library patrons and rifled through the card catalog.

materials

Rusted tins (see page 19)

Small conduit strap

Small nails

Baby spoon

Photocopy of vintage photo

Text paper

Mica

Small metal frame

Jeweler's epoxy

Head pins

Pearls

Wire

Silver beads

Round tin with clear lid

Jewelry cable

Crimp beads

Magnetic clasp

process

1 Jane cut apart a full-sized mint tin with a jeweler's saw. There are several ways to accomplish this, so choose the method you feel most comfortable using. Be forewarned: The cut edges of tins are sharp! Jane created safety edges on the cut tin by folding over the edges with a special tool. You can accomplish the same task by smoothing the cut tin edges with a metal file or rubbing them against a piece of scrap wood wrapped with sandpaper.

2 A small conduit strap forms the bail for the pendant. First, Jane drilled small holes in the top rim of the cut tin. She threaded small nails up through the holes of the tin and the conduit. Then Jane used pliers to bend each nail end back to form a loop.

3 Jane wanted to slip the spoon handle through the miniature tin. She used a handheld rotary tool outfitted with a cutoff wheel to make slits in the top and bottom edges of the tin.

4 Two holes were drilled in the center back of the miniature tin. Jane then placed the smaller tin inside the cut half. She marked and drilled the holes in the cut tin. Jane used cut nails as rivets to fasten the two pieces together. Using eyelets would work just as well (see page 21).

5 Jane photocopied a vintage tintype (see page 13). She mounted the photocopy onto text paper, topped it with mica, and placed the entire assembly into a small metal frame found in the scrapbooking aisle of a craft store.

6 The spoon was slipped back into the tin. Jane determined the frame's placement on the spoon. She removed the spoon and drilled holes in both the spoon and the frame. Jane then placed the

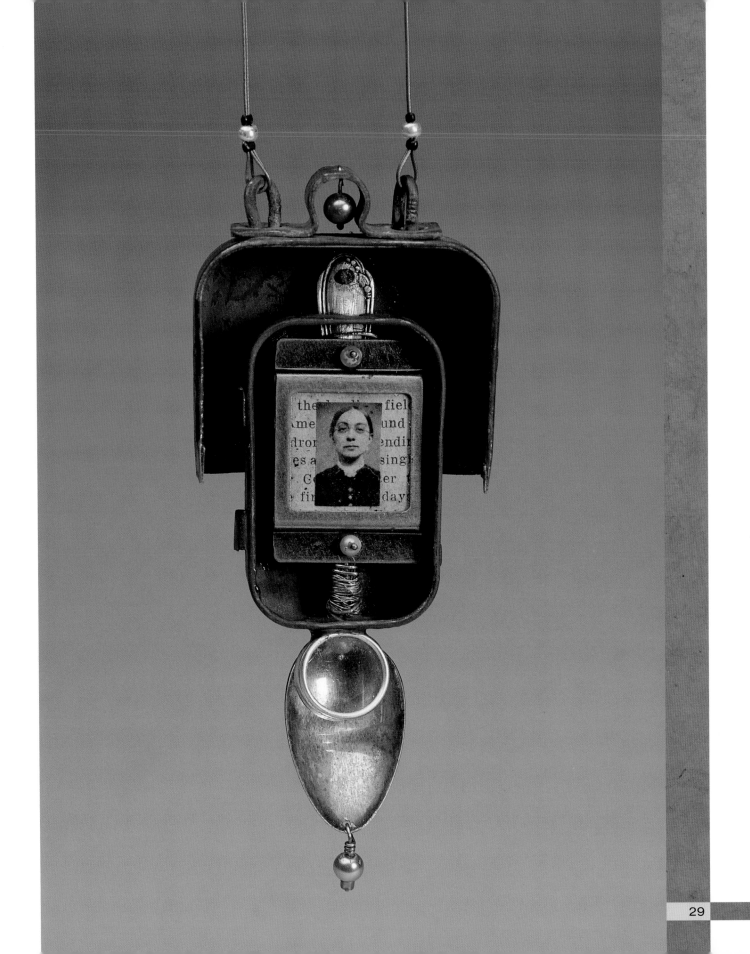

Rust and tarnish inspired this piece! These wonderful little rusted mint tins, along with a tarnished spoon, were enough to delight my senses when I created this odd sculptural pendant.

Jane Wynn

spoon back in the tin. She spread a small amount of epoxy on the frame, carefully aligned the drilled holes, and adhered the frame to the spoon. After the epoxy set, Jane threaded a head pin with a pearl, slipped it into one of the drilled holes, and wrapped the excess wire around the spoon handle. She repeated the process in the opposite hole with a second head pin.

7 Jane drilled a tiny hole in the aluminum lid. She threaded a pearl onto a head pin, placed it inside the lid, and used the excess wire to make a small, flat loop on the lid. The lid was epoxied to the bottom edge of the tin.

8 A decorative, wire-wrapped bead drop embellishes the spoon. Jane drilled a tiny hole in the spoon's bowl and secured the drop to the bowl. For a bit of color, she epoxied a tiny jewel to the top of the spoon handle.

9 Jane used doubled lengths of bronze-colored cable, crimp beads, pearls, and a twist clasp to create the hanging strands for the necklace. Ribbon, twine, or recycled costume jewelry chains could be used for an entirely different effect.

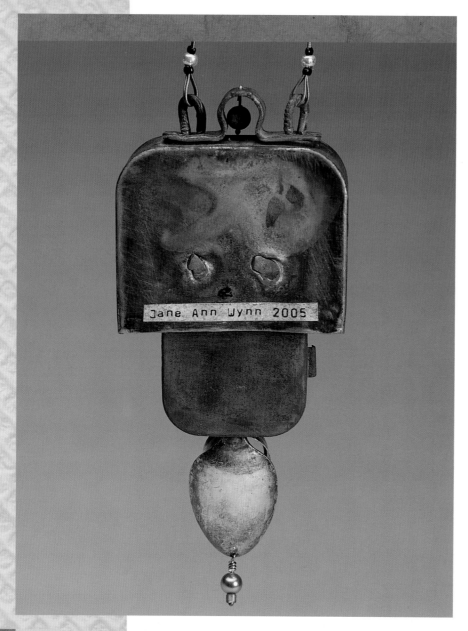

corporate greed

CREATED BY MARGERT KRULIJAC

Take a stand on issues of the day using visual expression. The creative act is capable of fuller and more persuasive expression than any words you might write or speak.

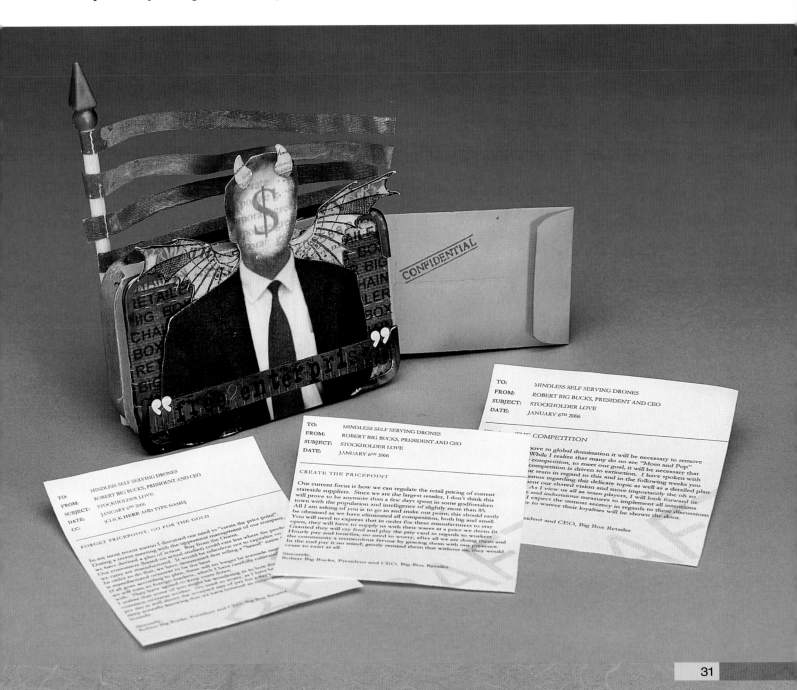

materials

Tin

Paper napkin

Matte acrylic medium

Transparency film

Acrylic medium

Decorative metal corners

Found imagery

Rubber stamp

Stamping ink

Acrylic glaze

Vintage metal ruler

Miniature flag

Miniature envelope

process

1 Margert removed the paint from her tin using a handheld rotary tool with a sanding-drum attachment. Then she marked a line along the side of the tin and used a cutoff wheel to create a slot along the marked line.

2 There are a number of ways to place patterns on a plain tin, including painting, rubber-stamping, and applying various metal finishes. Margert used the old, reliable technique of decoupage. She separated the layers of a decorative paper napkin—a pattern of red, white, and blue stars and stripes—and applied the top layer to the tin's lid with acrylic medium. The pattern was trimmed to the tin's shape after it had thoroughly dried.

3 Using a word-processing program, Margert typed the phrase "corporate greed" to create a pattern to superimpose on the striped surface. She simply copied and pasted this text over and over to create the pattern.

It's a good idea to play with a variety of font selections in your program. Try out a font, print it, then change the font and print again. Worst-case scenario: You wind up with a lot of scrap paper to doodle on. Once Margert settled on a font selection, she printed the text onto a clear sheet of transparency film.

4 Margert trimmed the printed transparency to fit the box lid. She glued the transparency to the lid at each of the four corners. Because the film is transparent, certain types of glue may be visible even when they dry clear. The decorative metal corners help camouflage the glued portions.

5 In keeping with the theme, Margert searched for imagery in order to create a Beelzebub of a "big boss." Once she found a suitable image, she erased the face of a business-suited figure and stamped a single image in its place. The figure was mounted on thin cardboard, cut out, and set aside.

Margert used a rubber-stamp image to create the wings and drew the horns freehand. An application of acrylic glaze on the wings and horns gives a sense of depth to these parts of the figure. After the glaze dried, the wings and horns were added to the figure.

6 The figure was glued to the front of the tin. Text was stamped on a section of a vintage metal ruler. The ruler, in turn, was glued across the figure.

7 Margert removed the small flag from the pole, cut the red stripes from the flag, and reattached the stripes to the pole. The pole was glued to the back of the tin.

8 A found image of an anonymous worker was cut out and applied to the back of the tin. Margert wrote the reversed text with a permanent marker. Her intent was to place the tin inside a mirrored display box so that a viewer could read the text easily while looking at the front of the box.

9 Margert created "secret documents" using her computer, and then sized them to fit inside the tin before she printed them out. These documents express her personal opinions about big box businesses and the "oh-so-sacred bottom line." To contain the documents, she stamped a miniature envelope with the word "confidential."

The inspiration for this piece came from a personal need to express my opinions in a creative form. This tin is a visual statement of my feelings regarding corporate greed and its effect on the working-class citizens of this country.

Margert Krulijac

eye above, river below

CREATED BY MICHAEL DE MENG

The vine-y, whorling form of the handle imbues this piece with a baroque presence. The all-seeing eye hovers above, emphasizing the extravagant use of ornament.

materials

Vintage drawer pull

Tin

Wire

Washers

Acrylic modeling paste

Wood

Vintage imagery and text

Gel medium

Acrylic paint

Found objects

Text

process

1 Michael's approach when he begins a piece is to gather objects and images together—he refers to it as a "large pile of things"—that he may or may not use. When Michael chose the drawer pull, it seemed logical to him that he wouldn't be needing the tin lid, so he removed it.

2 Thinking ahead, Michael pierced two small holes in the back of the tin. He threaded a short length of wire through the holes and twisted the ends together to create a hanger for the piece.

3 Michael glued two metal washers to the back of the tin to soften the rectangular shape. As Michael positioned and repositioned various items

on the tin, he noted that the large washer's circular form echoed the curve of the drawer pull. He aligned the pull and glued it in place. Michael found that the area where the back of the drawer pull met with the side of the tin was jarring. To disguise this area and make the joint appear seamless, he spread a covering of acrylic modeling paste over the area.

4 A roughly cut (and perhaps slightly charred) piece of wood was glued inside the tin. Adding the wood served to push out the collage elements that he envisioned using from the back of the tin.

The collage elements were added after the glue had dried. Michael used gel medium to adhere both photos and text. Michael admits that he was "not very tidy" with his glue application because he knew he would alter the piece later with paint and other materials to make it appear aged.

5 Michael applied acrylic paint to the piece, tinting objects and adding designs. (In all his work, he experiments with paint as he works.) The strange vine forms on the top of the piece reminded him of seaweed, so the color scheme he had originally envisioned started to shift in that direction. Blues and greens started

to become dominant, and symbols of water seemed to emerge "pardon the pun, out of the blue."

6 Thinned washes of acrylic paint were brushed onto the piece to unify disparate objects. Michael keeps his washes—typically gold or black—watery and translucent, adding layer after layer to darken the surface.

7 Once the piece was covered with washes, additional objects and images were added: the oval tin with the "mermaid" figure, the all-seeing eye, and pieces of text. Final layers of wash were added to the piece as needed.

Full fathom five thy father lies;
Of his bones are coral made;
Those are pearls that were his eyes;
Nothing of him that doth fade,
But doth suffer a sea-change
Into something rich and strange.
William Shakespeare, *The Tempest*

This is my favorite Shakespearean quote of all time. It's not only a reference to mortality and the flimsy, transient nature of flesh, but also, in my humble opinion, a manifesto for the assemblage artist. All things suffer a sea-change; assemblage artists just expedite the process. Our goal is to transform the mundane into something sublime. A toaster, with an artist's touch, can move beyond its role as a bread burner and become a thing of communication and inspiration. The old life lost but not forgotten. Now it is merely a reference point in its distinctive position as a piece of art.

Michael de Meng

"Something that has been worn over time or loved has more juice, and that translates into the finished work. You gotta like that."

Lynn Whipple
Owl Girl, 2005
10⅝ x 7¹⁄₁₆ x 1 inches (27 x 18 x 2.5 cm)
Collage, drawing and assemblage using found image, altered with acrylic and ink, found objects, antique paper
Photo © Randall Smith

LYNNE WHIPPLE WAS BORN and raised in Winter Park, Florida, a small, beautiful, liberal-arts college town, with a lot of lakes, great-looking oak trees, and brick streets. Her mother, Lynne says, is and was a great influence on her. "She has [an] incredible sense of style and great taste, and is an amazing artist." As Lynne was growing up, her mother was an English and creative writing teacher, so their house was filled with books and art.

Her grandmother also had a strong influence on Lynne's future work. One of Lynne's favorite memories is of spending time with her grandmother. "We would spend hours together at her dressing table, going through all her old photos, letters, jewelry, gloves, hankies, perfumes, and the stories that went with them. I never tired of this. I was fascinated with her personal history. She was a lovely person, who adored birds and played the piano. She had a great impact on me, and surely it translated to my work."

Lynne thinks of herself as a true mixed-media artist—one who makes use of many different techniques, materials, and ideas in her work. "I believe in complete freedom to try things," she states. "My work has evolved over time, but [it] still has the flavor it had from the beginning." She describes that work as a combination of collage, drawing, painting, assemblage, sewing, photography, and the use of found objects.

Among Lynne's favorite artists are Paul Klee and Jean Dubuffet. She has always loved Klee, both for the childlike quality of his art and for his great sophistication and intelligence. Dubuffet appeals to her because of his fearlessness and his willingness to express concepts freely. "He doesn't care if it's pretty," Lynne says. "His work always makes me laugh." Lately, Lynne has also been impressed with Tim Hawkinson, whom she thinks of as a genius. "We saw his show at the Whitney last year. It had big ideas, was very ambitious, and it made me laugh."

What triggers Lynne's artistic visions? "Anything can spark a piece. I find inspiration everywhere." Her ideas, she explains, come from materials, certain photos, music, drawings, conversations, deadlines, dreams, found objects, nature, writing, accidents, traveling, and just playing around in her studio.

Sometimes, Lynne's ideas for a piece come to her as soon as she finds a perfect object. She knows before she even gets home exactly how the piece will be and how she'll finish it. "I also have tons of ideas in progress. Pieces and parts." Lynne finds this ongoing process—"all the starts and threads of thought that eventually will be tied up"—quite amazing. While she believes that the mind is always solving problems, she thinks that her hands also lead her to solutions. For Lynne, the studio is just a space to experiment—a laboratory of sorts—in which she can let her imagination run amuck.

Lynne's working methods vary. Sometimes, she starts with sketches, but more often her work is prompted by handling her materials. "I really like to think with my hands. It's almost as if your mind goes on autopilot, and [the work] just happens."

Lynn Whipple
Cat Face, 2005
8¹¹⁄₁₆ x 7¹⁄₁₆ x 3/8 inches (22 x 18 x 1 cm)
Collage, drawing and assemblage using found image, acrylic, found antique paper
Photo © Randall Smith

Lynn Whipple
Gift, 2005
7¹⁄₁₆ x 9⅞ x ⅝ inches (18 x 25 x 1.5 cm)
Collage, drawing and assemblage using found objects and images, antique paper, string
Photo © Randall Smith

37

These days, her favorite technique—the simplest and most satisfying—is collage with paint and drawing.

Her finished pieces don't always look the way she envisions them when she first starts out. Some have a tendency to evolve. In fact, Lynne says that they "seem to have minds of their own. Sometimes they boss me around, but I am satisfied when I can keep [them] simple and still surprising."

Lynn Whipple
Good, 2005
6¹¹⁄₁₆ x 5½ x 1¾ inches (17 x 14 x 4.5 cm)
Collage and assemblage using found objects and fabric, antique paper
Photo © Randall Smith

Lynne is an avid collector of many items for her own personal pleasure. She loves finding and wearing what she calls "cheap, cool plastic or weird rings. You know—stuff with style, but lowbrow." She's also fascinated by good-looking old tambourines and odd musical instruments. "I have the coolest banjolele and weird handmade drums and percussion instruments. I just started a project on collecting laugher—taped and photographed."

For her studio, the list of what Lynne enjoys collecting is very long indeed, and includes "old photos, more old photos, photos, tintypes, letters, books, paper, boxes, bottles, metal stuff, old stuffed animals, rocks, stuff from nature, leaves, fabric, threads, jars"—any objects, Lynne says, that look as if they will tell a story, objects that are red, and "just cool, old stuff."

Lynne likes to work with found objects because they

"I believe in complete freedom to try things."

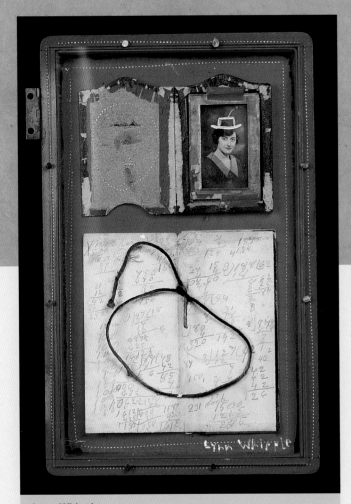

Lynn Whipple
Untitled, 2005
11 x 6¹¹⁄₁₆ x ⅝ inches (28 x 17 x 1.5 cm)
Collage, drawing and assemblage using found objects, acrylic, antique
paper, string
Photo © Randall Smith

Lynn Whipple
Nice Hat, 2005
11¹³⁄₁₆ x 5¹⁵⁄₁₆ x ⅝ inches (30 x 15 x 1.5 cm)
Collage and assemblage using found image, antique paper, string
Photo © Randall Smith

have past lives, they're a little beat up, and they have "some great story that we can only imagine." She's intrigued by the mystery of the objects' paths through time. And the objects' imperfections make them all the more interesting and real to Lynne. "Something that has been worn over time or loved has more juice, and that translates into the finished work. You gotta like that."

John Christopher Borrero
Saraswati: Ballad of the Dyslexic Band, 2004
35⅞ x 12 inches (91 x 30.5 cm)
Found objects, metal, wood, doll parts, photograph, printing blocks on wood panel
Photo © Peter Wolf Photo-graphics

JOHN BORERO, WHO IS NOW A TRAINER for Head Start in Boston, was raised by Puerto Rican and Dominican immigrants in a multifamily railroad-style apartment in Brooklyn, New York. He lived in many states and in Germany before he earned a bachelor's degree in psychology from Wesleyan University in Connecticut, and moved to Boston to pursue a life as a psychiatric social worker.

Formal training in art never entered the picture for John; his interest in art arose during what he describes as a "childhood spent with my head in the clouds, developing my imagination while avidly collecting comic books." He began creating art as a way of using the materials that he found around him, and has experimented with a few different techniques but always returns to using unaltered artifacts and old "undiscovered" items.

John enjoys Gustav Klimt's pieces and the way in which Klimt's characters never seem to fit on the canvas—as if their essences were too large to be captured. He also enjoys how Klimt's pieces encourage viewers both to step back and take in the whole image, and to move in close and appreciate the detail. John endeavors to create the same effect in his own pieces. He's also drawn to Edward Gorey's perspective. "He saw...the shadow in every instance of lightness." John greatly admires Tim Burton's vision and the stark beauty that Burton sees "in people and places that are a little dark and in those beings that are sometimes about to fade from our world." Burton's attention to the often unnoticed character is something that John shares.

John also admires the Thai artists who produce beautiful wooden wall sculptures that can be as large as an entire wall, and that are detailed enough to portray events that take place across an entire village. These sculptures allow the viewer to absorb the enormity of an artist's vision, but also invite the viewer to move in closer and enjoy the everyday details of life. The sculptures are difficult to

ship, burdensome to mount, and
expensive, but if John could own
any art that he liked, he would
choose one of these wall pieces.

John says, "Each of my pieces
begins with a story to be told—a
story that perhaps hasn't been
given a nuanced rendering in the
past—or with a character whose
sense of usefulness would
benefit from a retelling.
There are women who are
not simply sinners but
virtuous, given the right
perspective. There are
events that, given a
less biased perspec-
tive, might have served to express all of the
present characters more fully. It is my goal to
engender this open, compassionate perspective
in my pieces."

John Christopher Borrero
Atropos, 2004
13¾ x 13¾ x 11¾ inches (35 x 35 x 30 cm)
Found objects, doll parts, old chair seat,
metal, glass, branches, photograph
Photo © Peter Wolf Photo-graphics

The story always comes first with John. Poems written by his friend
Dane O'Hara have inspired several of John's pieces. He also credits
Dane for having "taught me to connect the well of my artistic expres-
sion to that of my spiritual expression. The day those sources were
joined was momentous for me." When he created the portrait of
Saraswati, the Hindu goddess of literacy, Dane's "Ballad of the
Dyslexic Bard" inspired him to create a divine being that could be a
guide for a dyslexic man who loved words.

A few days after reading this poem, John started to search for the
components of this goddess. All he knew at first was that he wanted to
create a being of compassion and grace who could love people in all
of their imperfection. The rest came on its own. John stumbled upon a
box of old printing blocks outside of an old factory building and walked
them home. It only took a few days for the piece to come together.

At any given point in time, John has ideas for 25 to 30 pieces. "Those
ideas call me into the studio, but once there, I most often find myself
working on something that wasn't at all sketched." John works on two
to three pieces simultaneously. Usually, at least one of them is a surprise to him.

Not all of John's studio time is productive. This frustrates him, but he
keeps going back. "One day, with persistence, the invisible cork

John Christopher Borrero
Aphrodite, 2004
24 inches (61 cm) tall
Found objects, photograph, wooden block
Photo © Peter Wolf Photo-graphics

John Christopher Borrero
Pandora's Jack-in-the-Box, 2004
9 x 9 x 18 inches (22.9 x 22.9 x 45.7 cm)
Found objects, discarded box, metal, wire, teakettle, music box, photograph, doll parts
Photo © Peter Wolf Photo-graphics

John Christopher Borrero
Black Madonna, 2004
47½ x 36 inches (121 x 91.4 cm)
Found objects, wood, metal, architectural details, old clock face, doll part, photograph
Photo © Peter Wolf Photo-graphics

trapping my inspiration will pop, and I'll engage in a marathon [creative] streak that will see the production of three to five pieces in a two- to three-week-long period."

When John's pieces come from pure inspiration, they come quickly. When he attempts to do pieces based on show topics, he barely meets his deadlines. "I'm usually one of the last entrants."

John feels that he has just scratched the surface of the technique he uses now—working with found-object sculpture placed onto solid wood panels. "My challenge to myself has been to try to accomplish as much depth of emotion as possible with as little manipulation of the found objects as I can permit."

John's pieces are never what he expects them to be. Early in the creation process, he sees himself steering away from his original vision. "I then try to follow the piece where it leads me." He has to work through the period of self-doubt that always intervenes. After that, he follows his feelings, stepping back every half hour or so to look at what he has. At some point, he finds that the piece has life and personality that it didn't have a few minutes earlier. "I'll feel a difference, and I'll feel pleased. I know it is done when it can speak."

John doesn't collect organic items, except for wood, but he does collect old, worn, and rusty items. He searches for artifacts that may already have enjoyed full lives and stories, and tries to give them something new. For example, he collects pictures of people who've already passed on and tries to "... give them a new identity through art."

Several years ago, John's world changed: he found new meaning in familiar items. "I found myself suddenly aware of nuances and shapes in nature. Tree branches looked like hands and bits of metal looked like faces." His manner of exploring and understanding this mystery—his way of coping, really—began with the found objects themselves.

"What follows logically for me is that my art is also rooted in my deep love for archeology, anthropology, mythology, and theology." In his work, most of which centers around revisionist accounts of history and folklore, John tries to engage the viewer with stories that speak to the human condition. "That's why many of my pieces speak to feminist characterizations and women's journeys. Above all, I hope that my pieces bring to mind the vulnerability of the human experience and the importance of loving that which is imperfect. If, in the end, I can help people to see the world around them with even a little more understanding, then I'll be pleased."

John Christopher Borrero
What She Saw, 2003
24 x 24 inches (61 x 61 cm)
Wood, glass, metal, doll parts, photograph on birch panel
Photo © Peter Wolf Photo-graphics

43

Teresa Petersen
Game Box With Red Bird, 2004
11 x 5½ x 2 inches (28 x 14 x 5 cm)
Vintage backgammon box, game boards, game pieces, toys, collage
Photo © artist

As a child, Teresa Petersen was usually at the dining-room table, coloring, playing with clay, or doing the craft project of the day. "Thankfully, I was always well supplied with art materials! There was a real 'do it yourself' ethic around my house, so I learned that philosophy—and the basic skills needed to do things like rewire a lamp, refinish furniture, make a box, sew a skirt, and make art."

Teresa majored in biology and painting/illustrating at Michigan State University. After graduating, she worked part time illustrating fossil reptiles, and rented studio space where she could make fine art. At that time, she was primarily painting, and her subject was often women in historical and outdoor contexts—figures inspired by vintage photographs and magazine advertisements. To frame her paintings, Teresa used old doors and windows from a junkyard behind her studio.

Teresa later received an M.F.A. from Wayne State University in Detroit, Michigan. During this time, she continued painting. She soon found that she had more fun using the wood from the doors and windows as art materials rather than simply as frames. She also started to use the vintage pictures that she had previously used only as references.

Working as a scientific illustrator had taught Teresa to appreciate the beauty of old magazine illustrations. "It's so much faster and fun," she says, "to find the right picture than to have to draw it from nothing!" For Teresa, painting ended up being a needless extra step—a less direct way to create the meaning she was after. Now, most of her pieces are assemblages and collages.

Recycling junk makes sense to Teresa, not only from an ecological standpoint, but also because junk links her art pieces to a time when people saved and utilized every scrap. The overlapping of history, women, culture, nature, and mythology is an ongoing theme of great interest to her.

For her collages, Teresa uses found scenes, such as paint-by-number paintings or thrift-store prints, as backgrounds. To populate these, she cuts out people, animals, and objects from old

"It's so much faster and fun," she says, "to find the right picture than to have to draw it from nothing!"

books, magazines, and catalogs. For her assemblages, she uses found objects—typically household items—as raw materials. She takes them apart and refits them with other objects to create new three-dimensional wholes.

Teresa likes Greek vase paintings, Japanese prints, and the works of Edvard Munch, Andy Warhol, and many surrealists because they tend to be very graphic and the space depicted in them is simplified. Her own works follow these styles. She particularly likes the works of Joseph Cornell, but for different reasons. With just a few, very simple objects, painstakingly chosen from the larger "real world" of things, Cornell, she says, "managed to convey to the viewer a glimpse of his personal world, all contained in a small box."

Teresa has been influenced by several living artists, among them James Rosenquist, Mike Kelly, Wayne Thiebaud, Betye Saar (see page 80), Raymond Pettibon, and Detroit artist Tyree Guyton. Teresa states that much of these artists' work is simple and graphic with bright colors. She enjoys their use of images and items from popular culture, and the manner in which they usurp the meanings of items for their own use.

For Teresa, a piece often starts with a particular object that strikes her as especially well suited to starting the telling of a story. "I have a bank of basic ideas and themes that I often use in my

Teresa Petersen
Blue Sky and Blue Water Game Box, 2005
17¾ x 13¾ x 5½ inches (45 x 35 x 14 cm)
Found box, game boards, game pieces, toys, collage
Photos © artist

works and a collection of materials with which to build pieces. One key piece—sometimes a newly found item, at other times something seen in a new light—usually works as a catalyst to bring an idea together with a number of other parts from my shelves." And "sometimes a different theme, a new experience, or a good opportunity forces me to look at the things I already have in a new way, which [begets] new ideas."

Usually, as soon as Teresa has an idea that she's excited about, she starts on a piece right away. A few of her ideas languish, waiting for the right time; some eventually get dropped from lack of sustained interest.

"I will often work on a series of things in batches of four or more," Teresa says. She may have five collages all laid out and work on one for a half hour or more, then the next, and so on, as ideas come and go throughout the day. She glues and frames them all at the same time, which is quite efficient because she can concentrate on one procedure at a time.

Teresa usually starts with a fully conceptualized idea for one portion of a piece—the core section that includes the special "catalyst" piece. Although she'll sometimes draw a quick sketch, she usually relies on the image in her mind, and creates the rest by trying out items to see if they fit together visually and thematically. She builds around the catalyst piece in layers, fitting more objects into the artwork and increasing its complexity. "The work is finished when the story that I imagined is there, and the work looks visually whole."

Teresa never knows exactly what a piece will look like until it's finished. When she starts a piece, she has a more complete idea of the story she wants it to tell than a vision of its finished appearance. She says that she's never happy with some of her works; she either sells these inexpensively to get them out of her studio or takes them apart again. She's quite smitten with some of her pieces when they're new, but later sees their flaws. Only a few favorite pieces hold their appeal for her—the ones in which all the pieces came together "correctly".

Although Teresa tries not collect things that she can't use, she admits it's a losing battle. She's inherited the collecting bug from both sides of her family. Vintage clothing takes up a lot of space in her house; she collects it because it's wearable, so it serves a function. In many of her artworks, she uses vintage pictures of women wearing the same types of clothing that she collects.

Teresa Petersen
Lady in Red Game Box, 2005
13¾ x 9⅞ x 4¾ inches (35 x 25 x 12 cm)
Found box, game boards, game pieces, toys, collage
Photo © artist

"The work is finished when the story that I imagined is there, and the work looks visually whole."

Teresa Petersen
Types of Clouds Golf Tee Game, 2005
19⅞ x 7½ x 2 inches (48 x 19 x 5 cm)
Golf tee game boards, tees, collage
Photo © artist

"I will often work on a series of things in batches of four or more..."

Detroit, where Teresa now lives, is steeped in history, and she reports that there's "a lot of good old stuff to make art out of." She can usually find what she needs on a curbside. If she doesn't find it on trash day, she goes to a thrift store. She collects furniture and interesting pieces of wood or metal to build boxes and structures for her works; outdated pictures for use as background scenes; and pictures cut from old books, magazines, and catalogs to populate the scenes. She reuses picture frames for finished artworks; wooden boxes and drawers for dioramas; and games, game pieces, and toys to make new game artworks.

"Working with found objects," says Teresa, "is fun precisely because the objects come with intrinsic meaning; they aren't blank like paper. I can subvert that original meaning by taking objects apart, breaking them into smaller bits of symbols, then mixing up those symbolic pieces with other things—possibly unrelated or unexpected but somehow right." Teresa believes there is an aspect of meaning that comes from way the work is created. "Cutting things apart and symbolically recreating them is part of the charm and power of collage and assemblage. It's like you are really changing the world, in a way, since you are changing real, everyday things from the world!"

Teresa Petersen
Black and Green Lotto Game Box, 2005
16⅞ x 13 x 3¾ inches (43 x 33 x 9.5 cm)
Found paint box, game boards, game pieces, toys, marbles, collage
Photo © artist

Ah, Sweet Mystery

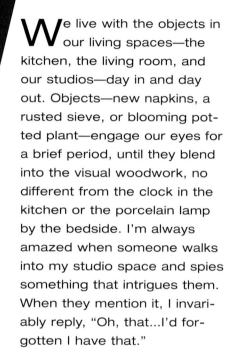

We live with the objects in our living spaces—the kitchen, the living room, and our studios—day in and day out. Objects—new napkins, a rusted sieve, or blooming potted plant—engage our eyes for a brief period, until they blend into the visual woodwork, no different from the clock in the kitchen or the porcelain lamp by the bedside. I'm always amazed when someone walks into my studio space and spies something that intrigues them. When they mention it, I invariably reply, "Oh, that...I'd forgotten I have that."

Sometimes renewed attention to an object is like discovering an object for the first time. I really love it when I see how I can use something I've had sitting around for a while (re: months or years) in a new art piece. Even more, I enjoy shopping with no purpose other than to just go look at things. (I can roam for hours in an antique mall and am more than happy to plop down on the floor to look through boxes of small trinkets or photographs in

small antique stores.) It's thrilling when I find an object I've never thought about using before, and have a clear image of how I'd like to use it.

Now, imagine that an unexpected package arrives in the mail for you. Inside is an object you've never seen before. Wouldn't it be a wonderful surprise? Would you immediately start thinking about what you could do with it or to it?

I wanted to try and create that feeling of discovery for five artists. I chose items that they had some experience with: wood, tin, fabric and paper. It might have been more interesting to send them something to work with that was totally out of their comfort level, but what I wanted them to experience was the arrival of something they hadn't been looking at in their workspaces every single day for the last year (or three). And I wanted to see just what they might come up with.

What would they do with the objects they'd been given? I gave them absolutely no parameters as to what or how they could use the object.

(That's not quite true: I did tell Bobby Hansson that he had to use the baby cup I sent him in his assortment of decorative tins.) Jen Swearington, a fiber artist, worked on two little-used, printed tea towels that I found in a drawer at my parents' house. I urged Susan McBride to do something with the wonderful cardboard object she had stored in our photo studio. Michael de Meng received the most mysterious piece in the mail and opened it on his return from a trip (see below). And just to make it interesting (as well as for expediency's sake) two artists chose their own object to work on and sent it to me as a surprise.

Using objects as the starting point for a small work of art (or a large one, if you wish) requires us to really look at and think about an object. Are you attracted to its shape or the qualities of its surface? Do you want to exploit the uniqueness of the shape or impose your own vision on the piece? What personal experience have you had with that particular object? Does it elicit a common response from others? Will this object help you tell a story or prompt a thoughtful response? Thinking carefully about these things will help you create work of your own.

Each of the five artists in this chapter have responded to an object in his or her own way. They have used techniques—painting, working with tin, working with fabric—with which they are familiar. Be prepared to be inspired and amazed by the inventiveness of each artist's approach to creating a new piece of art.

Jen Swearington
Tea, 2005
27 x 14 inches, (68.6 x 35.5 cm)
Vintage tea towel, acrylic paint,
thread, batting

adjust-o-matic

CREATED BY SUSAN MCBRIDE

Restraint and a sense of graphic élan informed this piece.
Often, less is more.

materials

Vintage dress form
Acrylic paint

process

1 It would have been easy to simply cover the entire dress form with images. The unadorned form itself was both a strong and compelling sculptural piece. Susan respected the inherent beauty of the linear pattern markings and was intrigued by the construction of the form—the cut shapes and how they were joined together. She didn't want to obscure those elements, so she chose to add only a couple of figures.

2 For this piece, Susan chose a color palette from the colors and fashions of her early 1960s childhood. Right before she agreed to work on the piece, she and I had been working together on a book—*Artful Paper Dolls*. The vintage imagery in that book, with which we worked every day, also influenced the visual style of the fashions she drew: shirtwaist dresses, heels, hair with a flip, and a pillbox hat.

3 Susan lightly sketched three figures on the form: two on the front and one placed diagonally on the back. She colored them with light coats of acrylic paint.

Rather than obscure the manufacturer's name on the form, Susan decided to draw the eye to the logo by highlighting it with white and ochre acrylic paints.

I retrieved this vintage cardboard dress form from a dumpster behind the building where I work. It lived in my house for several years, on top of a dresser or perched on a chair, until my husband very politely asked if it could please go live somewhere else. He didn't like it very much. However, Terry loved it and pleaded with me to work on it for this book.

The dress form's shape—enhanced by the darts and tucks—reminded me of the dresses my mother wore when I was a little girl. I have memories of fashion illustrations in the Sunday newspaper. All those breezy, long, whimsical women confidently rendered and done up in flowered, flowing, and tailored frocks, with shoes and bags to match, made quite an impression on me.

Susan McBride

harley kin

CREATED BY BOBBY HANSSON

I sent "Professir" Bobo a box full of decorative tin cans and a vintage baby's cup. My only stipulations were that he had to leave the cup intact, and he must use it in the piece! An inveterate punster, Bobby has played with both visual and verbal puns in this figure.

materials

Decorative tins

Wood block

Brass nails

Wire

Screws

Screw hooks

Baby cup

Belt buckle

Metal stamps

Acrylic rod

process

1 Bobby spent a lot of time just eyeing the tins. He arranged them on a shelf and occasionally added a piece or two from his personal stash as he waited for them to speak to him. The tin with a diamond pattern (on the legs) drove him to his dictionary. He found two definitions. One was "a legendary troop of demon horsemen: in medieval Latin, the hellequini," the second, "a mischievous buffoon wearing parti-colored tights." The demon horsemen made Bobby think of tattooed bikers. He decided that his figure would have oriental tattoos (courtesy of tea tins) on his chest and arms.

2 A simple wooden shape forms the torso of the body. Bobby nailed on tin shapes cut to the shape of the form.

3 The arms and legs of the figure are simply constructed. Basically, they are formed from simple rectangles, with tabs placed at either end. Bobby rolled the rectangles into tube shapes and then used a household soldering iron to run a line of solder down each seam.

Heavy wire was threaded through the tabs between the arm and leg pieces to enable them to move freely. The arms are screwed to the torso; the legs hang from screw hooks.

Holes were drilled into the wood form of the torso and the base. An acrylic rod inserted in the holes allows the figure to stand with the arms and legs swinging freely.

4 Bobby is a metalsmith (among many other things), so he created the face of the figure by using techniques with which he's familiar. He used repoussé techniques to create the facial features. Have you ever drawn a line on a piece of aluminum foil and then turned it over to find an embossed line? In repoussé, you work on metal from the back, using special tools to push out designs on the opposite surface.

5 The baby cup was altered only slighty—it was crushed together to fit on the figure's head as a helmet. Bobby added an angelic belt buckle to the front of the figure. He used metal stamps to create the title of the piece on the arched, tin patch on the back of the jacket.

The tin with the
diamond pattern in
the box of tins Terry
sent to me triggered
a memory of those
medieval guys with
diamond tights.

Bobby Hansson

bette davis eyes

CREATED BY LINDA AND OPIE O'BRIEN

Linda and Opie were on their way to Mexico to teach when they agreed to do a piece for this book. I offered to send them something while they were gone, but they suggested a sorpresa for me, instead.

materials

Found objects

Vintage shoe last

Beach brick

Dowel or stick

Screws and nails

Epoxy (wood and concrete)

process

1 Always the hunters, Linda and Opie wrote that "beachcombing on Lake Erie provided the mouth, formed with a rusted jar cap and brass garden hose nozzle."

Linda and Opie are frequent denizens of the recycling plant in their area. Here they discovered the copper-wire hair (part of a discarded generator) and the embellishment on the top of the head (a discarded sprinkler cap and bottle cap).

Garage-sale castoffs contributed a vintage token for the nose, electrical fuses for the eyes, a metal flame, and the upholstery tacks.

2 Bette consists of two separate parts: a head (the shoe last) and a base (the beach brick). A hole was drilled in the heel of the wood form and in the beach brick. Linda and Opie joined the two pieces with a timbale stick ("timbale" is the French word for "timpani"). The stick is not secured with glue. This makes the piece very portable and easy to ship in a box with a bit of padding.

3 All of the embellishments were attached to the wood form with small screws, nails, or wood epoxy.

How-to Tip

Allow your drill bit do the all the work: Use light pressure and don't force the tool. Diamond-coated drill bits should be used on hard materials such as stone or china. Drilling through hard materials creates heat, which will cause china and stone to crack. In order to avoid creating heat, you'll need to cool your bit as you work. Have a container of water close at hand and dip the drill bit to cool it off as you work. Masonry bits should be used to drill holes in bricks. And always wear protective eyewear when you're drilling hard materials!

We loved our shoe last and didn't want to cover up the natural aged patina on this unique shape, which surely developed over the entire career of the shoemaker. Leather formed over the wood, random spills of leather dye, and even the nail marks added to its aesthetic appeal. There was no doubt for us that the shape was figurative in nature. It was predestined to become the foundation for a new "recyclabot" head. She's got those eyes...

Linda and Opie O'Brien

first-aid collage series

CREATED BY JEN SWEARINGTON

Jen created two distinct and separate pieces with the pair of vintage tea towels I sent her. Though the pieces are similar in many ways, Jen's personal artistic vision is most evident in the small quilt she made for herself with one of the towels.

In both the quilt and the collages, I was inspired by both the function and the printed patterns of the tea towels I was given. In the collage pieces, I forced the large patterns into small compositions, which made the cropped flowers bold elements in the collages.

Jen Swearington

materials

Vintage tea towels

Furring strips or canvas stretchers

Fabric scraps

Thread

Gesso

Acrylic paints

Vintage imagery

Acrylic medium

process

1 Inspired by the floral patterns of vintage tea towels, Jen decided to make small works that would utilize the patterns as bold elements of the composition. Jen built three 6 x 6-inch (15.2 x 15.2 cm) frames out of furring strips on which to mount the cut fabric. Don't want to build frames? Canvas stretchers—look for them in art-supply and craft stores—will serve the same purpose.

How-to Tip

Depending on the size of your frames and towels, you may need to piece the towel with other fabrics in order to reach the desired size for a second or third frame. Simply use a sewing machine to attach pieces of other fabrics to the remaining towel pieces.

2 Jen used the frames as viewfinders or templates to help her decide where to cut the tea towels. This allowed her to play with different pattern compositions before she cut the fabric. When she chose a composition, she cut out the fabric larger than each frame's dimensions. This allowed her to wrap the fabric around the edges of the frames.

3 Before Jen mounted her fabric on the frame, she created additional design elements in her composition by stitching contrasting scraps onto the fabric and adding machine-stitched lines—straight, zigzag, and curved. Hand-stitching could also be used to achieve a similar effect.

4 Each cut piece of tea towel was stretched over the frame. Jen recommends starting in the middle of one side and working from the center out, pulling the fabric taut against the frame. She used a staple gun to secure the fabric to the frame. Tacks could be used to create an entirely different look.

5 Jen painted around the printed floral patterns with gesso. After the gesso dried, she added color and line with acrylic paints, pens, and a pencil.

6 Vintage first-aid-manual illustrations were cut out and glued onto the fabric with acrylic medium. Jen hand-stitched around the illustrations.

7 Jen continued to layer paint, stitches, and a few more collage elements until she felt each piece was complete.

8 As a working artist, Jen creates both art quilts and wearables. When she received her mystery objects, I told her she only needed to make one piece with one of the towels, but she was so pleased with the material that she created one of her signature, small art quilts that combine drawing and painting as well (see page 49). Because her material was, after all, a tea towel, she painted a whimsical image of a tea party.

from earth to 5 flowers

CREATED BY MICHAEL DE MENG

Though the story behind this piece adds immeasurably to our enjoyment, what matters most is the striking use of the found object to create a haunting vision.

materials

Sleeve-pressing board (see page 49)

Nails and screws

Acrylic paint

Vintage text and imagery

Fan blade

Curved picture glass (2 pieces)

Hardware

Hinge and hasp

Vintage electric iron platen

Polyurethane adhesive

Fibers

process

1   To evoke the "grave-shaped hole" of the tomb entrance, Michael outlined the shape with small holes drilled into the top portion of the pressing board. Then he used a wood chisel to carve out the rough shape.

2   A row of common nails (echoing the stinging bee and other religious symbols) was added to the edge of the pressing board.

3   Michael added washes of acrylic paint to the board. Along the edge, dark streaks near the nails mimic trails of rust; on the chiseled hole, dark paint suggests burnt wood.

4   He glued a sheet of text to the base of the pressing board,— behind the cut-out shape.

5   The fan blade was attached to the base of the pressing board. Michael used washes of blue and green acrylics to give the metal a verdigris finish. The same finish could have been created with commercial solutions, but Michael's first love is painting—he feels more comfortable wielding paint and brush for his decorative effects.

6   Vintage text was cut out and applied to one of the curved glass pieces. The second piece was glued on top, then an image and more text were added. Michael fashioned supports for the glass with screws, bolts, and a hinge on the iron platen. Then the entire assembly was secured to the board.

As in all of his work, Michael makes liberal use of an industrial-strength polyurethane glue to adhere disparate items such as the glass and metal. And he freely admits that he isn't very neat in doing so because the surfaces will be given washes of acrylic paint to create the illusion of age. Look carefully at the curved glass pieces; the illusion of years of exposure to smoking candles or nicotine has been achieved with washes of acrylic.

7   On the pointed end of the pressing board, Michael wound threadlike fibers and tinted them with acrylic paint. The fibers give the piece additional textural interest. Michael tinted the fibers with acrylics.

8   Michael attached a rusted hasp to the upper portion of the pressing board and added a bit of text that brings to mind Roman numerals. Thin washes of acrylic paint help to unify the rusted metal with the entire piece.

Mexico is a strange and magical place. Whenever I'm there, I always feel like I'm surrounded by unseen forces—old gods, and new gods. Not long ago I returned from a trip to Oaxaca. I didn't know the function of the mystery object that arrived in the mail while I was gone, but I knew the subject matter that I would work with because my mind was focused on separate incidents involving me and a killer bee, and hundreds of flying insects.

My wife, Cindy, and I, along with a few friends, journeyed to an Oaxacan village called Zaachila to see some Zapotec tombs. One of my friends pointed out a Zapotec stone with the image of a jaguar on it. As soon as I went to look at it, I was attacked by a crazed, persistent bee. After multiple attempts to fly down my shirt collar, the bee finally managed to sting me on the back of my neck. I'm allergic to hornets and was slightly freaked out, so I popped a few antihistamine pills, just in case, and continued on to the tombs.

The tombs were small—not for the claustrophobic. Each entrance was a grave-shaped hole, with rock stairs leading down into the ground. On the tomb walls were images of two skeletal underworld deities wearing hearts around their necks. Each skeletal figure was accompanied by a priest: one was named 5 Flowers and the other 9 Flowers.

Afterwards we wandered up a hill that overlooked the ruins. The trees on this hilltop were covered with flying things—large wasp-like bugs (which made me a bit uneasy after my encounter with the crazed bee), as well as hundreds of butterflies. The insects buzzed and fluttered in a swirl of activity from tree to tree. For me, it was a bizarre combination of danger and beauty, not unlike life.

I really didn't reflect fully on this incident until I sat down to work with my mystery object. I wanted to combine the strange mixture of feelings I experienced. I wanted to create something that represented the mysterious priest 5 Flowers, the tomb, and the concept of rebirth. By the time I was finished, I wondered if there was any correlation between the jaguar stone, the killer bee, and 5 Flowers. Was my experience a message, a warning, or a blessing? After all, bees have been viewed as messengers of the gods in many cultures. I don't normally think this way, but I'd just returned to the United States. My American skepticism hadn't had enough time to wash away the mystical dust of Mexico.

Michael de Meng

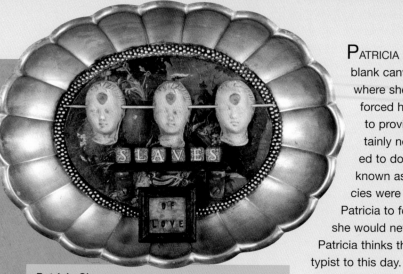

Patricia Chapman
Slaves of Love, 2003
11¼ x 15 x 2¾ inches (28.6 x 38.1 x 7 cm)
Tray, print, pearls, wax, rusted metal brackets, shelf, wooden cubes, frame, polymer clay, mold, brass heart charms, skewer; adhered, constructed, stamped, drilled, glued
Photo © artist

Her artistic tendencies were alarming to her mother...

Patricia Chapman
Sleepless in Santa Fe, 2005
25¾ x 22¾ x 6½ inches (65.4 x 57.8 x 16.5 cm)
Wood, molding, acrylic paint, acrylic glaze, wax, peg board, vintage book, metal disk from antique music box, map, glass, clock part, vintage chalk ware figure, metal charms, bed springs; constructed, painted, sealed, adhered, carved, coated, drilled, wired
Photo © artist

PATRICIA CHAPMAN WONDERS if the relatively blank canvas of the flat Midwestern landscape where she was born and raised may have forced her to develop an imagination—just to provide some interest in her life! She certainly never had to question what she wanted to do; even in grade school, she was known as the class artist. Her artistic tendencies were alarming to her mother, who told Patricia to forget about art and learn to type, or she would never be able to support herself. Patricia thinks this may be why she's such a poor typist to this day.

As soon as she was able, Patricia moved from Nebraska to Berkeley, California, where she finished high school and attended the Academy of Art University in San Francisco. Eventually, she moved to Phoenix, Arizona, and gravitated to the crafts department at Arizona State University. While she was there, she focused on working with textiles, creating large-scale, sculptural wall pieces made with a wide variety of fibers. After she left ASU and moved to California, she began working with art consultants on both coasts, creating fiber sculptures on a commissioned basis for public spaces.

Patricia has always loved Matisse for his joyous use of color and graphic sensibilities. Another of her favorite artists is Joseph Cornell; he will always have a special place in her heart for having ushered in the use of found objects in art. Her list of admired contemporary artists is long. On it are Keith Lo Bue, whom she admires for his fabulously detailed assemblage and jewelry—"brilliant universes of invented history"—and for using the discards of humans and the natural world. She also likes Robert Rauschenberg, for having redefined the word "painting" with his use of found objects and appropriated imagery; Alexis Smith, for her glorious use of found objects and ephemera, and astute use of text to create humor and irony; Luis González Palma, for his powerfully dreamy and soulful photo images; Leighanna Light, for combining found objects to create demented macrocosms and wacky characters; and Darlene McElroy, for her exquisite mixed-media paintings, romantic and nostalgic imagery, profusion of textures, and found objects.

Patricia's art germinates from many sources. Often, a single object will lead her to a concept. Sometimes the concept arises from a combination of acquisitions—either as the result of an accidental juxtaposition or of a more conscious juggling act. At other times, she comes up with a concept first and then has to find the right objects to illustrate it. She also finds it inspirational to work within the parameters of a certain show theme; this offers her the chance to explore subjects that she might not ordinarily investigate.

Patricia has never been able keep up with all the ideas she has for new work. Several months may pass before she can get around to the actual production of a given piece. But she points out that there's a benefit to working this way: her idea has time to marinate and refine itself, and the elements of a piece can be added, subtracted, or altered.

Typically, Patricia works directly with the objects she plans to utilize in a piece, shuffling the ingredients until she's satisfied. In the case of a concept that's born before she's found the objects to represent it, Patricia makes a rough sketch of the concept first. If the work will reside in one of her constructed boxes, she creates a box pattern, sizing it to fit the contents exactly.

Choosing a favorite working technique is almost impossible for Patricia. Making her art is a heavily process-oriented endeavor. Because she works with such a wide variety of objects and combines them in such a wide variety of ways, each combination of objects in her individual pieces presents its own challenge in terms of adhering, bolting, or wiring those objects within the piece or to each other. Patricia frequently alters her objects by drilling, sawing, painting, or applying a wax coating. One of the only consistent aspects of her art is the construction of the boxes that she makes for so many of her pieces. "I think I may be genetically predisposed to carpentry, because my

Patricia Chapman
Ignorance Is Bliss, 2005
20 x 6 x 6 inches (50.8 x 15.2 x 15.2 cm)
Porcelain bust, alphabet blocks, vintage coffee can, fiberboard; cut, brushed, adhered
Photo © artist

Typically, Patricia works directly with the objects she plans to utilize in a piece, shuffling the ingredients until she's satisfied.

Patricia Chapman
Insight Sucks, 2000
18 x 18¼ x 5 inches (45.7 x 46.4 x 12.7 cm)
Wood, molding, acrylic paint, wax, printed segments, plywood, bottom of a
metal spring form pan, segment of vintage lamp fixture, curtain ring, frame,
silver-leafed plastic wings with threads, bird's wings; constructed, painted,
sealed, printed, attached
Photos © artist

Patricia Chapman
Waiting, 2005
17⅜ x 18⅜ x 4 inches (44.1 x 46.6 x 10.2 cm)
Wood, molding, acrylic paint, acrylic glaze, wax, Kraft paper, paper, photos,
glass, brackets, vintage scientific specimen holder, vintage plastic figurine,
plastic men; constructed, painted, printed, dry brushed, coated, adhered
Photo © artist

grandfather was a master carpenter…Sometimes people will ask me where I found the boxes for my pieces because the way that I finish them gives them the look of age that corresponds so well with the age of the objects in them."

To a great extent, curiosity about what a finished piece will look like is what motivates Patricia. But she confesses that there are times (fortunately not many) when she's dissatisfied by the reality of the finished work. If she can't rework a piece, however, she has no regrets about taking it apart and using the components in something else.

Over the years, Patricia has collected figures of hands, several of which have worked their way into her art. "I think I'm drawn to the hands because of the importance that my hands have in expressing myself. Not only in the creation of my art, but in the way I 'talk' with my hands." She also acquires figurines that she can use as main characters when presenting a narrative about some aspect of the human condition. Other powerful members of her found-object cast are toys, animal figures, dolls, frames, trays, and a huge potpourri of wood, glass, ceramic, metal, and plastic objects.

Patricia's favorite sources for objects are flea markets, and her favorite is the one by the Port de Vanves in Paris. The flavor and age of the objects she finds there are very different from what she finds at home. When the concept for a piece precedes the acquisition of the object she wants, she sometimes turns to online sources. Patricia also has a team of friends who act as surrogate scavengers for her and who have kindly given her some marvelous treasures.

Patricia finds it especially gratifying to utilize found objects that have a rich patina of history—things that have somehow survived because they've been deemed worthy of survival. That fact, in and of itself, has a very potent metaphorical value to her. The hunting and gathering process is critical to the evolution of her art, and she

Patricia Chapman
A Stitch in Time, 2005
21⅝ x 12½ x 3 inches (55 x 31.8 x 7.6 cm)
Wood, molding, metallic paint, wax, paper, vintage clock glass
faceplate, porcelain doll hand, rhinestone, vintage image, pine,
metal, clock hand, rug needle, fork tines, vintage frame; constructed, painted, coated, adhered, printed, cut, drilled, stitched
Photo © artist

loves how the found objects within her work can
transport her to wherever she was when she
found them. "I love the intuitive and emotional
relationship I have with the presence and personality of these objects. I find that using the
rich symbolism and familiarity of objects with
the synergistic power of text to be a very powerful way to communicate."

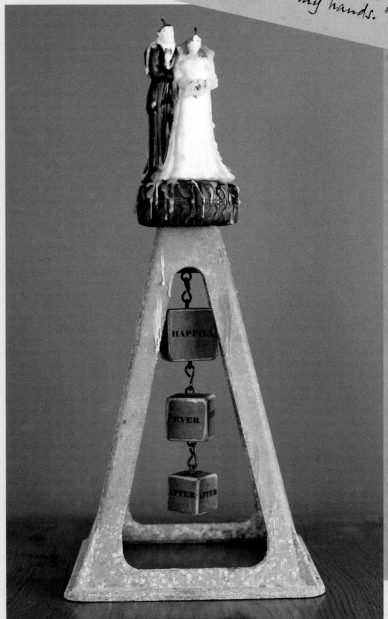

"I think I'm drawn to the hands because of the importance that my hands have in expressing myself. Not only in the creation of my art, but in the way I 'talk' with my hands."

Patricia Chapman
Happily Ever After, 2004
14 x 6 x 6 inches (35.6 x 15.2 x 15.2 cm)
Candle, toy wheel, aluminum, wood, chain; adhered, melted, printed, attached, hung
Photo © artist

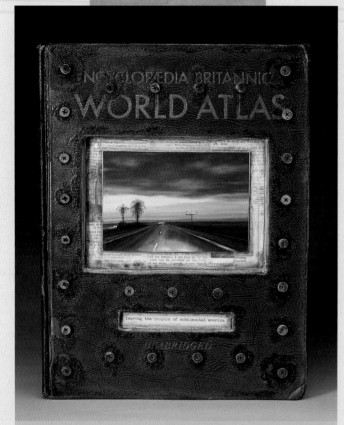

Joe DeCamillis
Leaving the Tropics of Continental America, 2005
15 x 11 x 1¾ inches (38.1 x 27.9 x 4.4 cm)
Mixed media

Like many other artists, his ideas can sit "around [his] psyche for years until all the elements necessary to execute them fall into place,..."

LOOKING AT JOE DE CAMILLIS'S WORK, it's not hard to see a connection to his greatest passion as he was growing up—reading. His favorite literary heroes—Jack Kerouac and John Steinbeck—were travelers and seekers, so just before Joe turned 21, he set off on his own solo journey from Boulder, Colorado, to southern California, where he studied creative writing at UCLA. Five years later, Joe put his attempts at writing aside for a while, and on a whim, learned the basics of drawing and painting. With his first oil painting, he felt right away that he could tell stories better with paint than with words.

As he was learning to paint, Joe restored a vintage RV and named her Lucy. He then set off on a three-year-long odyssey throughout the continental United States. Along the way, he sold hundreds of his paintings, developing his skills as an artist through the sheer volume of work necessary for survival.

As he traveled, Joe's habit of collecting odds and ends also started to escalate to its present state—obsessive-compulsiveness. Joe started collecting during his childhood, when he had recurring dreams about finding wooden chests overstuffed with precious treasure. "I tirelessly roamed the woods behind our house looking for those treasures—or at least a lost wallet filled with cash or a stack of faded girlie magazines." At one point, he collected hundreds of different empty beer cans during walks in his suburban neighborhood. The cans, he says, "gave me my first appreciation for the art of design... My first experience at layout and composition came from arranging my large collection in my bedroom." Now, his favorite places to hunt are along roads and footpaths, on beaches, and at flea markets and thrift stores. Like many mixed-media artists, Joe is attracted to "things aged beyond recognition but still maintaining much of their original form."

Joe credits his mother's artistic journey as a big influence on his work. As a child, he says that his favorite creation of

Joe DeCamillis
Classic American Adventure, 2005
16¼ x 12½ x 1½ inches (41.3 x 31.8 x 3.8 cm)
Mixed media

Like many mixed-media artists, Joe isn't faithful to a single favorite technique. If he were to pick one, it would "probably change before the week was over."

hers was a mixed-media collage, "back before mixed media was even a common label, let alone a buzzword." She made this collage for Joe's dad from scraps of building materials that she scavenged from the construction site of their first dream home.

His own artistic process is constantly evolving. His subject matter and style has changed from loosely brush-worked, simple, colorful compositions to dramatic scenes from the contemporary American Road, painted in the style of the Dutch Masters, on copper panels.

In 2004, Joe's work took a different course. First, he pushed the extremes of scale by creating paintings smaller than postage stamps. Not long after that, he built his first frames from old books. These frames emphasized the storytelling nature of his work and merged his passions for art, writing, and collecting. Within months, the books stopped serving as frames alone: they began a dialogue between collaged elements of text, imagery, and Joe's own personal writings.

Recently, Joe has started to paint on round pieces of steel and ceramic briquette, and to experiment with layering old pages and then sanding them down to expose fragments of

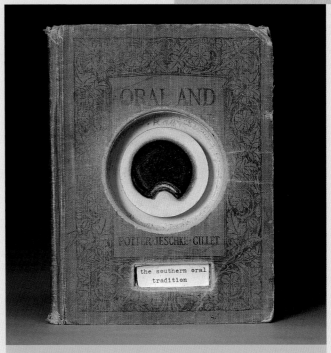

Joe DeCamillis
The Southern Oral Tradition, 2005
7½ x 5½ x 1 inches (19.1 x 14 x 2.5 cm)
Mixed media

65

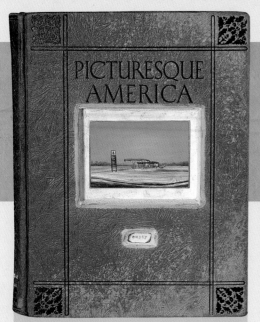

Joe DeCamillis
Empty, 2005
10 x 7½ x 1 inches (26.7 x 19.1 x 2.5 cm)
Mixed media

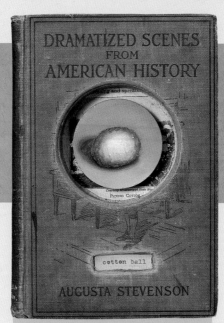

Joe DeCamillis
Cotton Ball, 2005
7½ x 5 x ¾ inches (19.1 x 12.7 x 1.9 cm)
Mixed media

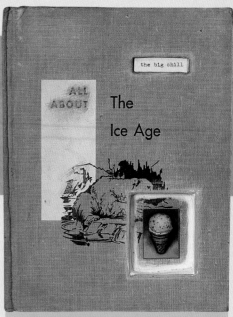

Joe DeCamillis
The Big Chill, 2005
9¼ x 7 x 1 inches (23.5 x 17.8 x 2.5 cm)
Mixed media

Found objects in his art evoke visual and physical sensations— connections to cultural relics and communal history that help viewers better experience his work by creating a personal connection to it.

the various layers of text and illustrations. His inspirations are the naked billboards that he photographs. He's drawn to the weathered layers of old ads that have been arbitrarily painted over, or that have faded or peeled away.

The names on Joe's list of favorite artists are not surprising: Albert Pinkham Ryder, William Blake, and Joseph Cornell (for their dark, visionary art and their working outside the "artistic academia" of their times); John Singer Sargent, James Whistler, Brueghel, Vermeer, and Rembrandt (for their mastery and intense talent); Leonardo da Vinci, El Greco, Emily Dickinson, Walt Whitman, and Marcel Duchamp (for being so far ahead of their times); and Eva Hesse (for her visual poetry). He's also drawn to contemporary artists such as Anselm Kiefer and Andy Goldsworthy (earthy and provocative, yet subtle and mysterious); Tom Friedman and Rachel Whiteread (clever and simple, yet calculated and thought provoking); and James Turrell (brilliant and complex).

Joe is a full-time, art-fair artist who shows in galleries as well. Showing at fairs and in galleries keeps him working under the constraints of deadlines. Like many other artists, his ideas can sit "around [his] psyche for years until all the elements necessary to execute them fall into place," a process over which Joe says he seems to have

Joe DeCamillis
Drive to Extinction, 2005
12 x 9 x 1¾ inches (30.5 x 22.9 x 4.4 cm)
Mixed media

little control. Once he's started his works, however, he completes them quickly and then turns them loose.

And what do Joe's pieces start with? "I go through life gathering found objects, digital snapshots of road scenes, my own life experiences, and personal observations of our culture, our society, and our history. I begin messing around first with one of the above four and then work the other three in until all four come together as a finished work of art."

Like many mixed-media artists, Joe isn't faithful to a single favorite technique. If he were to pick one, it would "probably change before the week was over." Currently, he's excited about layering old pages with acrylic varnishes and mediums, painting oils onto copper, and burning things (especially books!) with his torch.

Joe's finished works usually end up close to the way he imagined them, but he's sometimes surprised by an end result. "By the end, though, I have almost always worked out all the kinks and am very excited to show the work." Joe says that if he's displeased with a piece, a few days or weeks (or in rare cases years) of distance from it might be all he needs to see it is as a worthy and finished piece, or to see exactly what he needs to do to bring it to completion.

Though Joe is first and foremost a painter, he likes the way found objects give him a direct physical connection to his subject matter—a link to his past and heritage. Found objects in his art evoke visual and physical sensations—connections to cultural relics and communal history that help viewers better experience his work by creating a personal connection to it.

Joe DeCamillis
Stuck in a Ditch in Denver, 2005
11½ x 10 x 1 inches (29.2 x 25.4 x 2.5 cm)
Mixed media

enced. 5. Not dr
rozen up. 7. F
ublic. 8. With
asily understoc
ral. 10. Clear. 1
ccount. 12. Fre
Liable to attack
d with the mot
Clear space, on l
. Make open. 2

Nicole McConnville
Open, 2004
5 x 14 x 5 inches (12.7 x 35.6 x 12.7 cm)
Wooden drawer, photo, anatomical illustration, found writing, dictionary
definition, metal tine, gauze, thorns, metal lock, mica, beeswax
Photo © Steve Mann

NICOLE MCCONVILLE WAS RAISED, for the most part, in upstate New York. She describes herself as having been a shy introvert until she entered college, where she made a handful of friendships and branched out through an extensive network of pen pals and mail-art correspondences. "It was actually through these mail-art creations that I discovered book arts and was able to further explore the creative possibilities in various openings and enclosures. I relished the sense of anticipation and discovery between myself and the recipient." Nicole's creations became more and more elaborate and eventually evolved into three-dimensional assemblage constructions. Her college studies in both literature and the visual arts helped solidify her passion for the juxtaposition of written language and visual forms.

As an assemblage artist, Nicole feels that it's important to pay respect to those who paved the way. "For me, that honor should be bestowed upon the father of box-art himself—the enigmatic and innovative Joseph Cornell. His ability to create visual poetry through the skilled placement of salvaged objects, his clever use of composition and negative space, and [his] mix of playfulness and control never cease to give me a sense of childlike wonder."

Nicole also enjoys the collage and correspondence art of trickster Ray Johnson, who, she says, not only possessed a unique sense of visual play, humor, and cleverness, but also helped to turn the definition of art on its head.

Nicole McConnville
Fragile, 2006
6 x 6 x 3 inches (15.2 x 15.2 x 7.6 cm)
Wooden box, wooden frame, ornithological illustration, bird legs, photo, bird skull, fishing lure, metal disc, mica, beeswax
Photo © Steve Mann

"It was actually through these mail-art creations that I discovered book arts and was able to further explore the creative possibilities in various openings and enclosures."

Among contemporary artists, Nicole most admires Stephen and Timothy Quay (better known as The Brothers Quay). "Known primarily for their astonishing stop-motion-animation films, the aesthetic of these identical twins celebrates decay, cast-off items, dreamlike states, and inner workings of the mind. Their impeccable use of light and shadow, camera focus, and movement, combined with brilliant puppetry and ethereal sets, creates entirely unique visual worlds. Each frame of their films is a visual feast. The narratives are not always straightforward, the symbols and meanings not always clear; the viewer is left to explore the terrain with curiosity, wonder, and sometimes, unanswered questions."

Most of Nicole's work begins with a single image, whether it's an old photo with a face that that draws her toward it or an illustration with a unique visual quality. Nicole says that once that key image is in her hands, "the wheels are set in motion, and the game begins. I might jump to a certain object that simply fits just the right need. A background texture or color might then work its way into the picture. It's a dance, digging through collections of knick-knacks, placing, moving, and then shifting the growing composition yet again until the various elements simply feel right. This process can be immediate...or it can be a prolonged, thoughtful romance where pieces need to be wooed into agreement."

For Nicole, the real challenge is getting started—finding the right foundation upon which to build. But once she begins, she's eager to continue. "Just as I approach reading books, once that cover has been cracked open and the first page is read, I simply have to see it to fruition. My focus is on one art piece at a time, and I give that piece my undivided attention until it is finished."

Nicole McConnville
Stasis, 2006
5½ x 12 x 3½ inches (14 x 30.5 x 8.9 cm)
Wooden drawer, ornithological illustration, metal machine parts, metal heart, nails, bird feather, paint, beeswax
Photo © Steve Mann

Nicole McConnville
Bugbelly, 2005
6⅞ x 11¾ x 2½ inches (17.4 x 30 x 6.4 cm)
Wooden drawer, photo, astronomical illustrations, paint, beeswax, beetle, mica
Photo © Steve Mann

"It's a dance, digging through collections of knick-knacks, placing, moving, and then shifting the growing composition yet again until the various elements simply feel right."

Nicole sees herself as a tinkerer. Although she says there are exceptions, she rarely knows what one of her pieces will look like until it's finished. "I think it is that process of discovery that keeps me going back to my studio with a sense of excitement again and again."

Collage is Nicole's first and lasting creative passion. The placement of objects, images, and text offers her an endless sense of possibility. "And when collage makes use of found and salvaged materials—that's when things get really interesting for me. The concept of taking that which is lost or discarded and giving it new life and meaning is at the core of what drives me as an artist."

Because Nicole doesn't work with a specific image in mind, she has nothing with which to compare a finished piece and is sometimes disappointed with its overall success. In fact, she's been disappointed enough to dismantle a piece completely after a couple years. "There have been times when I felt the piece didn't deserve to exist any longer and that the individual components would be better utilized if they were recycled into my treasure chest of materials. The first time I destroyed a piece, it was a bit shocking, but relief and satisfaction soon sank in when I realized that I didn't have to settle for what I viewed as inadequate work."

Nicole has a special fondness for old medical and anatomy books; she finds them to be almost sacred. "Open an old anatomy text and discover both the gorgeous and the grotesque. See the body deconstructed into a network of complex working systems—a collage of blood, bones, and flesh. What cuts to the core of our humanity more than images of the body? We are dichotomies of vulnerability and strength."

Among the many items that Nicole collects—from bones and machine parts to dead bugs and old jewelry—old photos are some of the most important to her. "Just look into the eyes of the face in an old image, and what do you see? A blank canvas or a lifetime full of stories? I think it's hard not to see a part of yourself staring back." Most of her photos are given to Nicole by people she knows. Some come from extensive collections or are gifts from people who have discovered her art and want her to transform something they have cherished into something completely new.

Nicole McConnville
Unlocked, 2005
6½ x 11¼ x 5¾ inches (16.5 x 28.6 x 14.6 cm)
Wooden drawer, photo, clock parts, tin can lid, key, mica, paint, beeswax
Photo © Steve Mann

Nicole McConnville
Honey, 2006
5¾ x 11½ x 5½ inches (14.6 x 29.2 x 14 cm)
Wooden drawer, photo, entomological illustration, mica, paint, beeswax
Photo © Steve Mann

Nicole McConnville
Blush, 2002
18 x 17½ x 3 inches (45.7 x 44.5 x 7.6 cm)
Cash register drawer, photos, medical illustrations, sheet music, beeswax, cotton gauze, machine part, silver milagro
Photo © Steve Mann

Nicole says that if you look closely enough, you can find real beauty in old, forgotten objects: a discarded wooden box, a rusted metal tool, the musty leaves of an old book. And "there is something innately powerful about rediscovering things that have been cast aside. I make art from the past. I seek out and collect images and objects that seem to have an interesting history or visual quality, and I give them a new voice. The pleasure is in the sense of discovery in the gathering of materials, the re-contextualization, and the process of creating a new environment."

71

James Michael Starr
King Me the Second, 2004
25 x 18 x 11 inches (63.5 x 45.7 x 27.9 cm)
Assemblage of chair, industrial clock, drill bits, tintype photograph,
door knob, drawer pull, toy wheel, bead
Photo © John Wong

JAMES MICHAEL STARR DISMISSES any formal art training he had as "so watered down as to be almost pointless. My real education came in my career as a graphic designer, where I feel I truly learned the elements of design and composition." After spending more than 30 years in the commercial art environment, James Michael started playing at making real art on his own time. In early 2002, he began working in his studio full-time.

James Michael has always worked with old, worn, or deteriorated objects from a relatively well-defined period in recent Western history—primarily objects manufactured between the middle of the 19th and the early 20th centuries. "I find distinct character not only in their present condition, but also in the original form, line, and color of these objects." He also gravitates toward them because he sees them—even if they're not recognizable—as somehow familiar to all of us in our collective consciousness.

Over time, James Michael has simplified his compositions significantly; he now limits the main components in any given sculpture to two or three. "This 'paring down' process began with limiting my collage elements to old black-and-white engravings and is now finding its way into my assemblages."

Although he feels that his work is a process of appropriation (he chooses not to create any of the components in a piece), until a year or two ago, he compromised by writing on most of his pieces. He hasn't done that recently, however, and may abandon the practice altogether. His inscriptions related to whatever the piece meant to him; now he finds it much more rewarding to let viewers interpret a piece themselves.

For James Michael, having a preconceived goal in mind when he begins a piece is invariably the kiss of death. Instead, a piece of his often begins with an extraordinary response to the beauty of an object. Sometimes he feels driven to begin working with the object right away, but James Michael will usually place the object on a shelf or pegboard—and wait.

"The mystery wrapped up in a beautiful old box or a head from a figurine has an appeal that is somewhat universal and even easy to understand."

The next step "is always about how that beautiful object might be complemented by another. This courtship usually takes place in my studio, where I keep as much of my inventory as possible in plain view." James Michael holds the inspiring object up to other things, or lays it on a table and pairs it with potential candidates. Sometimes this matchmaking will go on for weeks or months. Michael says that he leaves the objects "lying together where I can check on them from time to time to see how they're getting along as I work on other pieces. It's usually a bad sign if they don't hit it off right away…the longer a pairing sits without clicking, the less likely it is to become a new piece."

Physically sketching out an idea for a piece never works for James Michael. But he does "practice a kind of mental sketching and fiddling," during which he imagines detailed compositions. He's able to work out more of the issues in his mind than he can by sketching or handling the objects.

Although James Michael toys for a while with the first two or three initial components of a piece, he says that he often reaches the point at which he needs "to abandon caution, go past the point of no return, and actually begin assembling things." When he feels himself pausing at this precipice, he often recalls the words of Picasso: "Risk everything."

Although James Michael admits that his feelings could very well change in the future, his favorite technique at the moment is collage. "I'm fascinated by the simple poetry of a beautifully engraved image on a foxed and spotted old book page, and how in the context of a collage, it can seem to be reconciled with a long-lost lover from a page in an entirely different book."

James Michael Starr
Garden, 2003
64 x 20 x 17 inches (162.5 x 50.8 x 43.2 cm)
Assemblage of terrarium, table base, globe, plaster bust, doll torso, doll arm, curly willow twigs, twine, electrical cord
Photos © Harrison Evans

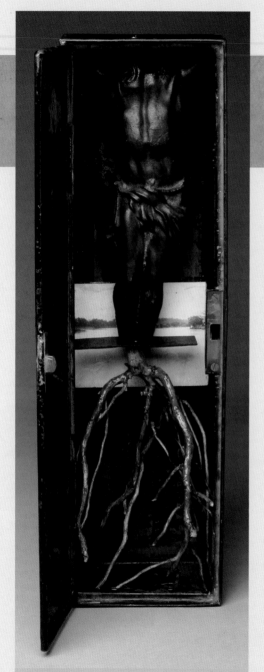

James Michael Starr
Potential Heir (detail), 2002
38 x 8½ x 8½ inches (96.5 x 21.6 x 21.6 cm)
Terrarium, iron ashtray, book page, illustrations, photographic print, ball bearings, brass ornament, watch part, document signature, fern leaf, construction toy parts, epoxy
Collection of Steve Ricketts and Caroline Waite
Photo © artist

In the future, he may increase the time he spends on assemblage. "The mystery wrapped up in a beautiful old box or a head from a figurine has an appeal that is somewhat universal and even easy to understand." For the time being, however, James Michael finds "the same intrigue lying just a little below the surface in these engraved images, and that appeals even more strongly to me for its subtlety." The relatively simple—and meditative—process of making these collages is part of their appeal to James Michael, as well.

Once he has matched up the first few components of a piece, a relatively complete mental picture of the finished piece springs into his mind, and the finished piece rarely varies much from that picture. James Michael works until he's satisfied that a piece is finished, but paradoxically, he's only rarely truly pleased with the end result. Setting a finished piece aside, delivering it to a gallery, or placing it in a collector's home where he won't see it for a while is sometimes helpful. "I will usually only later be able to look at it objectively and evaluate whether or not the piece was successful. But even then, I cannot say that I'm at all likely to be satisfied with what I did."

Because he's agitated by clutter—unless it's the slightly controlled mess in his work space—James Michael isn't much of a collector. "Such an attitude might seem contradictory to the art that I produce, which is all about 'things.' But as odd as it may sound, I don't even feel very comfortable surrounded by my own work." He does have a small collection of old crucifixes that he appreciates

James Michael Starr
Cohaesus, 2004
17½ x 5 x 4 inches (44.5 x 12.7 x 10.2 cm)
Assemblage of safe deposit box, cast iron corpus, artemesia plant, steel plate, photographic print
Photo © John Wong

James Michael Starr
I Complain to You with Pain and Sighing, 2003
7 x 4½ x 4½ inches (17.8 x 11.4 x 11.4 cm)
Assemblage of porcelain doll, tintype photograph, decorative brass leaf,
brass lamp part, text from German prayer book, epoxy
Photo © John Wong

"I will usually only later be able to look at it objectively and evaluate whether or not the piece was successful. But even then, I cannot say that I'm at all likely to be satisfied with what I did."

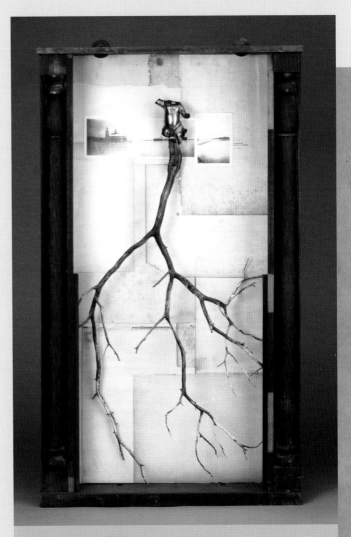

James Michael Starr
Dead To The World, 2004
30 x 17¼ x 4½ inches (76.2 x 43.8 x 11.4 cm)
Assemblage of clock cabinet, cedar branch, cast metal figurine,
photographic print, book pages
Photo © John Wong

for their iconic nature, as well as for what the cross means to him personally. He also collects old books for their engravings, typography, and aged pages. And he keeps a variety of containers in his studio, filled with three-dimensional objects. "My favorites are heads and body parts from dolls and figurines because most of my work revolves around the human figure in one way or another." To play supporting roles in his assemblages, he accumulates salvaged hardware, clock parts, other mechanical devices, and Victorian-era decorative objects.

James Michael enjoys working with found objects in part because as a graphic designer, he created what were essentially works of assemblage in their own right. He's attracted to the challenge of working within the narrow palette of his found objects. His goal is to bring these objects together into a whole that might contain more beauty than that of its individual parts.

75

Comfort

W hat is comfort? Is the word a noun or a verb? If you couple it with a noun, it's an adjective. What provides comfort to one person doesn't necessarily offer it to another. "Comfort" is a word that is loaded with personal connotations and associations, and subject to infinite interpretations.

When you work with an object to create a piece of art, you bring to it your own interpretations and feelings. You try to express these thoughts and feelings visually through your choice of object, as well as the materials, imagery, and text you use. These choices are thematic as well as visual in nature.

Sometimes you may find yourself working with choices that only later become thematically clear to you. "Oh, that's why I was drawn to those images of trees and those sketchy lines." At other times, you may start out with a clear thematic choice in mind.

To create this group of five projects, I asked four artists to work thematically with the word "comfort." What inspired me to

choose the theme was simple: I wanted to create a piece with a photograph I owned of a dapper gentleman tasting soup. I'd considered using the photograph for a year or two, but never got around to creating something tangible. Deadlines are powerful creative forces in and of themselves; they force us to get to the task at hand.

Working with a specific theme is a good exercise. It gives you parameters: You're forced to choose objects or images that readily convey that theme. Jean Moore used a small metal

headboard as her inspiration, while scraps of old barn board appealed to Sarah Urquhart. Nicole McConville was drawn to a first-aid box, and old photographs inspired Jane Wynn and myself. We each used different materials and some common techniques to create the works—and no two interpretations of comfort are alike.

If you were to work with the theme of comfort, your piece might contain elements similar to the ones in this group of projects, but it would be totally different from all of them. What does comfort mean to you? What do you visualize when you think about it? How do you choose the objects with which you wish to work?

When you've finished reading this section and savoring the rich variety of visual expressions, pursue the theme yourself. Wield the techniques you feel comfortable using to explore it. But don't run out in search of a metal headboard or a first-aid kit. Find something that speaks of comfort to you.

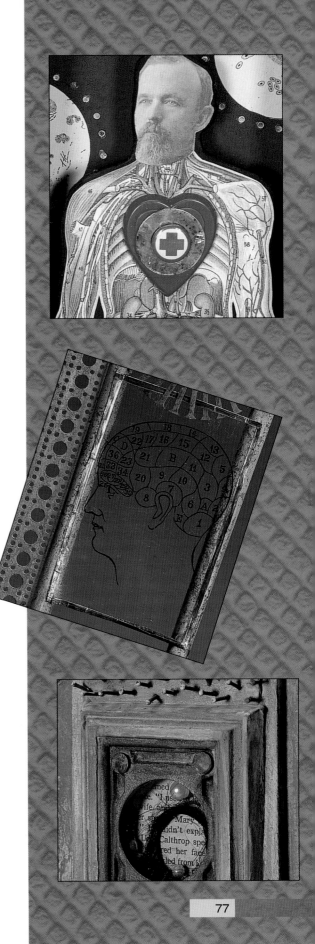

comfort triptych

CREATED BY SARAH URQUHART

Weathered wood, carefully selected objects, and simple forms tie the three parts of this triptych together. Visual restraint is often a virtue and expresses an idea more clearly than layers upon layers.

materials

Weathered barn wood

Thin wood strips

Plywood

Natural objects

Copper flashing

Book cover

Text

Cookbook

Found objects

Antique photograph

Glass

Small nails

Silicone glue

process

1 Sarah began this triptych by selecting the pieces of weathered barn wood that she would work with. She used a jigsaw to cut a peaked "roof" on each piece.

She wanted to create an inset box shape in each piece of wood. To do this, she outlined a shape on the wood. Then she drilled a small hole just to the inside of one of her marked lines. Next, she threaded a jigsaw back through the drilled hole and cut out the shape.

2 Sarah envisioned placing a piece of glass in each box shape in order to enclose the items. She needed to devise a way for each piece of glass to sit just inside the shape. She cut thin strips of wood, making them shallower than the depth of the box. Then she cut the strips to length and glued them to the interiors of her cut boxes.

3 Sarah cut out small pieces of plywood slightly larger than the box shapes to serve as backgrounds. She marked the outline of a box shape on each piece. Treating the plywood pieces as canvases, she painted or collaged elements onto each one.

X marks the spot on the first part of the triptych. Does it symbolize a hidden place on a map for exploration? Inside the box are tokens of the natural world—a butterfly wing and seed pod. Verdigris-coated copper flashing is fashioned into a roof for this piece.

The roof of the next part of the triptych is fashioned from a book cover. In the box, the background is a scrap of a handwritten recipe. A diminutive child's feeding spoon, skeleton key, and thimble are symbols of domestic life, as is the button inset in the barn wood.

An antique photograph creates a background for the family portion of the triptych. A house-shaped game piece is placed on a nail to make it seem as if it were floating inside the box. A scrap of text—the definition of "family"—and a simple metal heart are quiet embellishments on this portion of the piece.

4 Each plywood background was attached to the back of the barn wood with small nails. Sarah sealed each piece of glass into the box with a clear-drying silicone glue.

My husband and I brainstormed what the notion of comfort meant to us. Two clear ideas were family and home, hence the obvious "family" and "domestic" sections of the triptych. The third idea—"freedom"—came from me. I was attempting to pin down what was comforting to me about nature, art, and the fearlessness of exploration.

Sarah Urquhart

oh sleep! it is a gentle thing

CREATED BY JEAN TOMASO MOORE

Jean's inspired choice for the basis of her piece is unusual and yet, just right. Be open to any and every possibility as you choose an object, then allow the object lead you where it may.

materials

Metal bed

Vintage imagery

Transparency

Copper-foil tape

Acrylic paint

Eyelets

Found objects: watch parts, skeleton keys, and rusted chain

Wire

Pillowcase or doll's pillow

Text

Gel medium

Seam binding

process

1 Jean found this slightly rusted day bed at a yard sale. She was drawn to its openwork panel and its small size—smaller than a twin bed. To prepare the surface, Jean scrubbed it lightly with a dry abrasive pad to remove any loose flakes of rust.

A friend of Jean's welded metal supports to the back of the frame. These supports serve dual functions: they project the piece from the wall and provide a convenient hanging device.

2 Jean considered using several images from a 1920s health book that she owns. She selected just one to scan and print onto transparency film—an image of a man sleeping on a rooftop—which touts the advantages of sleeping in the open air. In addition, she scanned vintage phrenology diagrams of the various regions of the brain to print on transparencies.

The transparencies were outlined with copper-foil tape. The adhesive-backed tape was folded against both sides. Jean found the color of the tape "too shiny and coppery," so she brushed it with a light wash of acrylic paint.

3 In order to suspend the images on the frame, Jean punched holes in the transparencies and then set metal eyelets to strengthen the holes. Jean drilled small holes in the bed frame and used wire to hang the transparencies on the bed frame.

I chose sleep to illustrate what brings me comfort. For me, it is the only time when my brain is allowed respite from incessant inner chatter. I think about the moment right before falling into slumberland, when all is well with the world and the body is allowed to be at peace. I think about laying my head on a soft, feathery pillow and snuggling under a warm quilt. This is an ultimate "ahhh" moment for me that is both soothing and comforting. I realize the mind is actively dreaming while I sleep, but dreams can also be a source of comfort.

Jean Moore

4 Watch faces and cog wheels were glued to the bed. They represent the "blissful unawareness of the passage of time as we sleep." Skeleton keys, suspended on chain wired to the bed, symbolize the unlocking of doors to the subconscious during the dream state.

5 Jean fashioned a small pillowcase out of a full-sized pillowcase with hand-crocheted edging, and dyed it in a solution of strong, hot tea. This toned down the whiteness of the fabric, blending it into the composition.

She printed the word "dream" on a copy machine. Using the gel-medium transfer method, she transferred the word to the pillowcase. For Jean, the pillow is the ultimate symbol of the comforts of sleep: "soft and inviting, forgiving of the weary heaviness of my busy head." She suspended the pillow with seam binding.

6 A line from Samuel Taylor Coleridge's *The Rime of the Ancient Mariner (Part V)* inspired the title of this piece: "Oh sleep! It is a gentle thing, Beloved from pole to pole!" After printing out the letters, Jean used white craft glue to adhere the quote to the bed frame.

tasty

CREATED BY TERRY TAYLOR

This piece, with its graphic overload, is an anomaly for me. Most of the time I strive for restraint, adding as little as possible to a found object. But just this once, I allowed myself to pack as much information into the piece as I could.

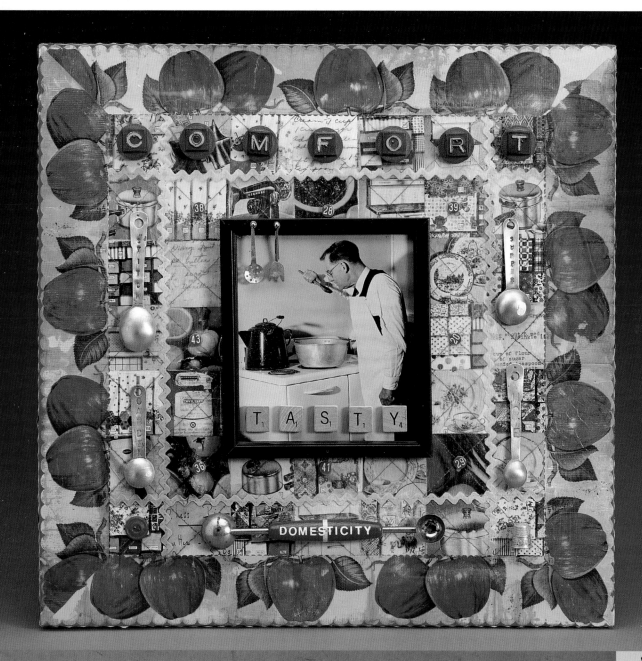

materials

Photograph

Found objects: melon baller,
teaspoons, tablespoons, and
numbered tacks

Imagery from a vintage
mail-order catalog

Vintage wallpaper border

Plywood

Acrylic paint

Japanese paper

Beeswax

Small screws

Rickrack

Game letters

Checkers

Adhesive lettering

How-to Tip

Always be on the lookout for useful materials. Craft and hobby stores stock miniature screws and nails, hinges, and other handy materials that should be added to your bag of tricks.

process

1 After a week of nonstop cooking on a beach vacation, a friend and I were shopping in an antique mall. Edith spied this dapper gentleman tasting his home cooking. He insisted on buying the framed photograph for me, with the proviso that I hang it up in my kitchen. And I did for a couple of years.

2 The first "alteration" of this composition began with the photograph itself. I happened to have the tiny kitchen utensils in my box of little things (see page 10). Tiny nails used by model-railroad enthusiasts attached the utensils to the wooden frame. Personally, I would have stopped right there, but I wanted to push myself further, just to see how far I would go.

3 I started looking through my vintage (circa 1960) mail-order catalog for domestic images: pots and pans, fabrics and rugs, dishes and vacuum cleaners. I cut them out and set them aside.

I found a length of scallop-edged wallpaper border. I loved the bright red apples and cheery yellow. I could picture this border on kitchen walls in the 1950s of my childhood.

4 A piece of plywood was cut to provide a base for the collage that I had started to imagine. I painted the plywood with acrylic paint.

The combination of the domestic imagery and the wallpaper border inspired a quilt background. I used a paper punch to cut out consistent squares from the catalog pages. Then I adhered the images in a checkerboard grid to clothlike

Japanese paper. Stitching—an old-fashioned domestic virtue—seemed like the proper way to embellish the grid and to add to its quiltlike appearance. I machine-stitched the grid with diagonal lines.

Next, I carefully adhered the stitched paper to the plywood, taking care to eliminate buckling. I covered the surface with waxed paper, weighted it with books, and allowed it to dry for a day or two.

5 I didn't have quite enough wallpaper border to edge the grid of images completely, so I photocopied the strip. This allowed me to miter the corners (as any good quilter would do) as I glued the border to the plywood.

The entire surface of the board was brushed with a coat of melted beeswax.

6 The photograph was attached to the board with small screws driven in from the back of the board.

7 A borber of rickrack lengths was laid on the board. I covered the rickrack with fabric and used a hot iron to adhere the rickrack to the waxed surface. Then I gave the rickrack a thin coat of melted beeswax.

8 I glued game letters to the checkers, and then nailed the checkers to the top of the grid. Self-adhesive letters were used to spell "domesticity" on the melon baller. Numbered tacks—used to match screens to windows in the days when screens were taken down or put up according to the season—were placed in alternating squares. Teaspoons and tablespoons completed the composition. As an added fillip, I used red thumbtacks to attach rickrack around the edge. Enough. More than enough.

I go to the beach for a week at Thanksgiving with a group of old friends. I begin to think about the evening's meal before I have breakfast (the only meal I don't cook). To my mind, the comforting combination of a hot cup of tea, a cookbook, and a view of the beach as I ponder the possibilities for the evening's menu is unsurpassed. Domestic pleasures of all sorts—cooking, stitching, embellishing (but not cleaning!)—give me a great sense of satisfaction.

Terry Taylor

altered first-aid kit

CREATED BY NICOLE MCCONVILLE

The restrained elegance of this piece appeals to me, as does Nicole's bold but understated use of red—the color of life.

materials

Vintage metal first-aid kit

Vintage anatomical illustration

Vintage photograph

Black mat board

Acrylic medium

Assorted imagery

Small block of wood

Mica

Vintage, heart-shaped plastic
   photo brooch

Red Cross button

Antique military braid

Metal tin lid

Text

Small glass bottle

How-to Tip

You'll get richer tones when you photocopy black-and-white photographs if you use a color photocopy mode.

process

1 Nicole painted the inside bottom surface of the first-aid kit to create a uniform visual surface.

2 The vintage anatomical illustration was photocopied to fit inside the box. Nicole also photocopied a vintage family photograph, sizing it to match the proportions of the anatomical illustration.

3 Next, Nicole carefully cut around the outlines of the photocopies. She positioned them on

I'd recently experienced a year filled with numerous family health issues. When confronted with the question of what one might define as comforting, the first thing that popped into my mind was the concept of healing energies, whether they stem from medicine or simply from the love and kind thoughts of family and friends.

Nicole McConville

mat board and glued them in place with a thin coat of acrylic medium. Once the glued images were dry, she sketched an outline approximately 1 mm all around the figure. Then she used a sharp craft knife to cut out the figure along the outline, and set the figure aside.

4 Nicole embellished the bottom of the box with a variety of illustrations culled from her collection of medical texts and dictionaries. She then glued the figure to a small block of wood before the entire assembly was glued in the box. This gives the vignette a sense of dimension and depth. The heart, mica, and Red Cross button were added to the figure after it was placed in the box.

5 The inside lid of the box needed a little embellishment. The original text was still intact. Nicole glued a length of antique military braid across the text, and glued a thin tin lid to the ribbon with epoxy.

6 Nicole cut out a dictionary entry containing the words "heal, healing, and health." She applied a thin layer of clear-drying glue to the small bottle and adhered the text to it. When the text dried, she glued it to the tin lid.

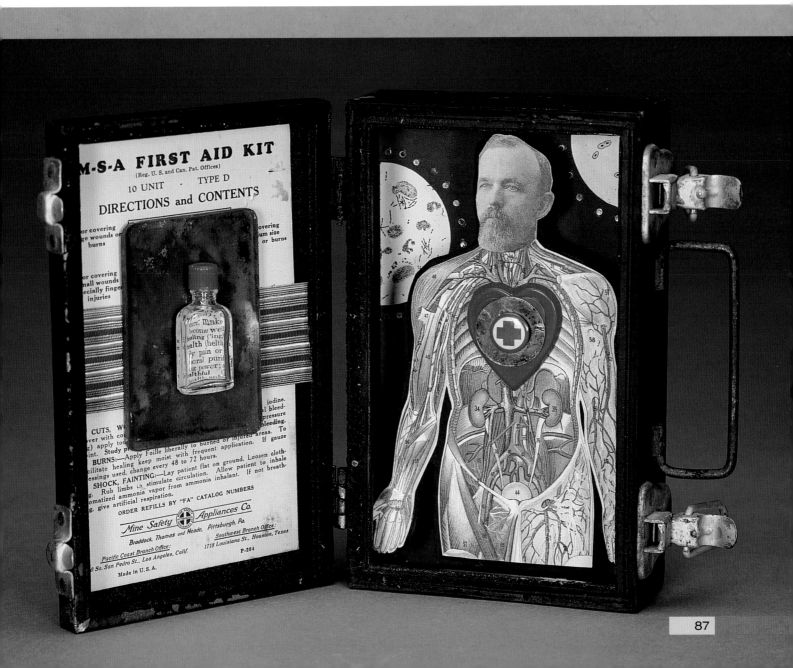

dog rider

CREATED BY JANE WYNN

In this piece, a discarded photographic image is transformed and given a new life by using an entirely different medium to recreate it.

The photograph of a little girl sitting on her dog made me feel so calm and nostalgic that I knew I had to find a way to share it. So I decided to paint it in a loose, brushy style with a limited color palette in the hope that I might create something that looked like the children's storybook images I loved as a child.

Jane Wynn

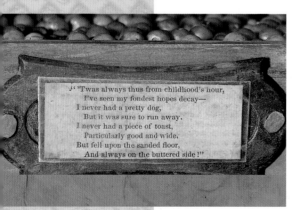

"'Twas always thus from childhood's hour,
I've seen my fondest hopes decay—
I never had a pretty dog,
But it was sure to run away.
I never had a piece of toast,
Particularly good and wide,
But fell upon the sanded floor,
And always on the buttered side!"

materials

Old photograph for inspiration
Small, prestretched canvas
Oil paints
Wood
Found objects: door plates, spoons, ruler, and pearls
Acrylic paints
Gold metallic paint
Wire
Patina solution
Text
Mica
Rubber stamps

process

1 Jane found the photograph on an online auction service. The photograph spoke to her. After winning the auction she "danced around for about three minutes and received the photo in the mail a few days later."

2 She sketched the image onto the canvas. Then she used oil paints to create her version of the photograph, in a style reminiscent of illustrations in children's books that she was fond of.

3 Using wood left over from the construction of her studio, she made a building-like structure to house the painting. Jane added a metal door plate and small wood strips around the top of the structure to enhance its architectural shape.

4 Jane gave the structure a coat of acrylic paint to seal the raw wood. Then she painted it with a metallic-based gold paint. When the metallic paint was completely dry, Jane coated it with a patina solution, which gave the paint a blue tint.

5 Old spoons were wrapped with wire and embellished with pearls. Jane drilled holes in the spoons and nailed them in place. Text was placed behind a sheet of mica, fitted into the door-frame plate, and nailed in place. A similar, smaller plate was added to the bottom of the piece.

Jane covered the bottom of the box with epoxy, then set tiny decorative pearls in place. She brushed them with a little bit of gold paint. When the paint was dry, she coated the pearls with patina solution.

6 The painting was attached to the structure with epoxy. Jane added some finishing touches to the surface: rubber stamping, a smidgen of an old ruler, and a bit of gold paint rubbed onto the wood surface.

The poem on the base plaque reads:

"'Twas always thus from childhood's hour,
I've seen my fondest hopes decay—
I never had a pretty dog,
But it was sure to run away.
Particularly good and wide,
I never had a piece of toast,
But fell upon the sanded floor,
And always on the buttered side!"

Janet Cooper
Assemblage Quilts 1-2-3, 2004–2005
10 x 16 inches (25.4 x 40.6 cm)
Vintage fabric and memorabilia

JANET COOPER GREW UP IN THE NEW JERSEY suburbs, and had the passionate fascination with New York City and Greenwich Village that feeds many a lonely suburban teenager in that area. Sociology was her major at Antioch College and the New School of Social Research. After graduation, she explored her developing interest in clay and combined it with community work by studying clay at Greenwich House Pottery in New York City and teaching in several community centers. Later, she taught classes in hand-building and alternative clay techniques at Greenwich House.

"I always appreciated and was intrigued by the precision and mechanics of women's work—sewing, crocheting, knitting, and quilting—but my medium (and love) was organic, flowing, impressionable, imprintable clay, which could be put together in moments with a slap, a pinch or two, or a spin on a wheel." In what Janet describes as her swan song to 20 years of clay work, she created an installation in 1986 that was essentially a clay flea market, enhanced with paint, cloth, and wood. Titled *Prairie Quilt I and II* and contained within a space of 20 x 10 feet (6.1 m x 3 m), this display was made up of smoke-fired and painted clay dishes, tiny dolls and figures, and barns and assorted artifacts made mainly of clay, but also of wood and cloth. Twenty years later, Janet now sees her fabric quilts as miniature flea markets—arrangements of various colors, textures, and treasures.

Much of Janet's clay work touched upon the human figure. She created porcelain heads and helmets, earthenware torsos, pots with the contours of human forms, and several series of dolls. Her attention—and obsession—next turned to bottle-cap art. Then she moved into tin-can work and made what she calls "Tin-Can People Pin Pendants" and "Statues." Her jewelry and craft work was sold in many galleries, including the American Folk Art Museum and the Museum of Arts and Design in New York, and The Society of Arts and Crafts in Boston. Her work has also been selected for several national exhibits including *Recycled/Reseen: Folk Art from the Global Scrap Heap* at the Museum of International Folk Art in Santa Fe, New Mexico.

Janet's work has changed over time, but the celebration of the human figure and her curiosity about the complexities of juxtaposition are threads that run through all of it. The box pieces that she creates today are sisters to what she formed in clay; she has substituted objects for what she used to model or pinch. And recently, she's returned to clay again. The *quilt ladies* are relatives to the torso and dress forms that Janet did in clay. "In my clay installation piece and other clay work that I did in the '80s, I'd already started to use fabric as an accent to clay, along with wood and paint."

Janet has admired and been influenced by Japanese design and craft ever since she first fell in love with clay. She admires the very early Haniwa figures and Bizen pottery, and is fascinated by *boro* (Japanese rag textiles) quilts. She has also been been inspired by most ethnic craft in clay and cloth, and since she first came across a Joseph Cornell piece, she's loved box art, too. Folk, outsider, and brut artists have influenced her greatly. Simon Rodia's *Watt Tower*, Grandma Prisbey's *Bottle Village*, and Reverend Finster's *Paradise* are all high on her list of favorite pieces, which also includes Michel Nedjar's cloth and bead dolls. Her first jolt of awareness of this obsessional use of materials came from seeing Clarence Schmidt's mirrored house in Woodstock, New York.

Janet's ideas come to her as she works, but nothing provides her with more focus than a deadline. One piece of work leads to another. As an example, several years ago Janet began making "visual scrolls" or panels, each about 8 inches (20.3 cm) wide and several feet in length.

"I have even taken sold pieces back to my studio to do a little more work on them. I work on pieces continually."

Janet Cooper
Quilt Lady, 2005
12 x 42 inches (30.5 x 106.7 cm)
Vintage fabric, assorted memorabilia, stitches and paint as decoration; hot glued

Janet Cooper
Assemblage Quilts 1-2-3, 2004–2005
18 x 22 inches (45.7 x 55.9 cm)
Vintage fabric and memorabilia

Much as a traditional quilter would do, she then combined or pieced a series of smaller squares into the panel. Soon, she started to combine the panels themselves into larger square shapes that resembled traditional quilts in their linear look. Now her quilts have evolved into somewhat restrained "crazy quilts," in that they are less linear and nonpatterned. Embroidery, laces, and stitches lifted from vintage textiles help subdue the squares. Recently this work evolved into "quilt ladies"—quilts crowned with heads.

Janet feels that her pieces are never completely finished, except perhaps when they finally leave her environment. "I have even taken sold pieces back to my studio to do a little more work on them. I work on pieces continually." She thinks of herself as lucky if she's pleased with a finished piece for a while, although a few pieces do give her continuous visual pleasure.

Janet may start a piece by making sketches, but these never resemble the finished version. She's usually working

Janet Cooper
Assemblage Quilts 1-2-3, 2004–2005
12 x 24 inches (30.5 x 61 cm)
Vintage fabric and memorabilia

on five or six pieces at a time. One of her favorite techniques is glue-gun work, which she likes because it's so immediate. Lately, she has enjoyed painting on fabric and using stitches as decoration for attaching.

Among the vintage objects that she collects are tin cans, tobacco tags, aprons, potholders, purses made from recycled materials, old catalogs, medical illustrations, crocheting and sewing samplers, hair jewelry, fabrics and textiles, purses, beadwork, buttons, folk art, dolls that are also purses, wallpaper sample books, and—of course—books. She also accumulates pieces of unfinished needlework, sewing baskets with their contents, old evening gowns, rugs, spools of thread, and glass jars filled with buttons. At one time, Janet had more than 35 bottle-cap baskets and a collection of 40-plus handmade cloth rugs.

Janet Cooper
Tin Doll, 2000–2005
4 x 14 x 1 inches (10.2 x 35.6 x 2.5 cm)
Vintage tin cans; snipped, punched, linked

Janet Cooper
Tin Doll, 2000–2005
4 x 11 x 1 inches (10.2 x 27.9 x 2.5 cm)
Vintage tin cans; snipped, punched, linked

Her work, Janet says, is less about recycling than about loving old things with vintage patinas. It's about arrangement and fabrics and objects, woven together with stitches. "I am so inspired by textiles: the printed fabric pieces of unfinished quilts, embroidered tea towels, braided and knitted rag rugs. These are my compulsions and visual excitements. My work does have something to do with recreating the spaces of my idealized childhood, invoking their intrigue and somehow trying to understand them."

"My work does have something to do with recreating the spaces of my idealized childhood, invoking their intrigue and somehow trying to understand them."

MICHAEL DE MENG SPENT MOST of his early life living in different areas of the West. His father worked for Xerox, so they moved frequently. His first memory is of a gecko. "We were moving into our home on Oahu, Hawaii. Behind the couch was a large window that looked into the yard, and on the window was a large gecko. Scared the living daylights out of me. Of course in time, like all people living on the Hawaiian Islands, I became buddies with these lizards, because more geckos mean [fewer] mosquitoes."

Michael made his first memorable piece of art in preschool. For Christmas, his teacher, who was also his mother's best friend, gave him colored markers and a plain white apron across the top of which she'd written "Merry Christmas, Mom." Michael proceeded to cover the apron with images of vampires and mummies.

Michael's parents were always very supportive. He had an endless supply of paper from his father's workplace and access to the copy machines there, which he thinks may explain his fascination with photographic imagery and collage. His obsession with eyes may be related to his grandfather's contact-lens business, where images of eyes appeared almost everywhere.

For the last 20 years, Michael has lived in Missoula, Montana, where he finished his art degree

Michael de Meng
Untitled Pez-Dispensing Totem, 2005
5 x 3 x 2 inches (12.7 x 7.6 x 5.1 cm)
Mixed media, found objects
Photo © artist

Michael de Meng
Untitled Pez-Dispensing Totem, 2005
6 x 2½ x 2 inches (15.2 x 6.4 x 5.1 cm)
Mixed media, found objects
Photo © artist

at the University of Montana. After graduation, Michael was exclusively a painter, influenced by German expressionist art and abstract expressionism. Artists such as de Kooning, Munch, and Kline weighed in heavily in his style. When he tired of this approach, his attention started to drift toward the stark, haunting, photographic elements of old silent films, including those of Melies and Eisenstein, and—in particular—Robert Wiene's *The Cabinet of Dr. Caligari*, in which the actors, with their severe black-and-white makeup, were placed into German expressionist sets. He liked this melding of photography and paint, and started to introduce photocopies into his large paintings.

During the first of many wonderful trips to Oaxaca, Mexico, Michael was "shrinalized"—a word of his own invention. "I also invented the term 'neo-shrinalist'; I consider myself to be one." Discarded items are plentiful in Mexico, but are often used in new and interesting ways. "I recall seeing a garden in which the owner had removed the filaments from 20 or more burned-out light bulbs, leaving only the glass forms, and had strung them along a garden wall. She then used them as little glass vases in which to grow plants. This amazed me. Here was a place where there was waste, but the waste was not wasted." Oaxaca also offered a plethora of shrines, which often incorporated nontraditional objects.

Michaels's art changed. He found himself working on his painting/collages in a very symmetrical way and incorporating shrinelike elements, such as arches. His pieces were still two-dimensional. Finally, he wearied of trying to create

Michael de Meng
Untitled Sardine Can Nicho, 2005
10 x 5 x ½ inches (25.4 x 12.7 x 1.3 cm)
Mixed media, found objects
Photo © artist

Michael de Meng
Untitled Sardine Can Nicho, 2005
4 x 2 x 1 inches (10.2 x 5.1 x 2.5 cm)
Mixed media, found objects
Photo © artist

the illusion of space in his work. "So I took a shovel (a very shrine-like form if you look at it with the handle toward the ground and the spade toward the top), and made a shrine from it. This was my first assemblage piece and my first experiment with neo-shrinalism." The piece led to the work he does today: using everyday objects to experiment with sacred forms and styles.

Michael's favorite artists are the social realists of early 20th-century Mexico, and include Diego Rivera, Orozco, and Frida Kahlo. "My first Mexican mural experience was Orozco's mural in the Instituto Cultural Cabañas in Guadalajara, which is often considered the Sistine Chapel of Mexico. The ceilings, walls, etc., are covered with his beautiful yet violent display of the trials of Mexico's inhabitants: slavery, despotism, and war. In many ways the term 'realism' is not quite the right word for this style because the work is so expressive." Michael avers that if he could have any work of art, he would love to own this mural. "Might take up most of my neighborhood, but that's okay. I'm sure I could find my neighbors a place to stay somewhere inside the structure."

Among the contemporary artists whom Michael admires are Jane Wynn and Nancy Anderson—assemblage artists and personal friends of his. Jane's work leaves Michael feeling as if he's discovered a strange and puzzling artifact from days gone by. He likes its mix of darkness and light, decay and beauty. Nancy creates assemblage shrines with, according to Michael, a heavy dose of kitsch and a great sense of humor.

The objects with which Michael works dictate the direction of the piece he's making. He doesn't plan his pieces in advance because he feels that planning doesn't allow for serendipity. He simply finds an intriguing object—and begins. Occasionally, he addresses themes, but even then, the piece is moved forward by the relationship of the disparate objects.

He usually tries to finish a piece once he's started it. "Nothing drives me crazier than an unfinished piece of work." Then, when he can pretend that it's finished, he goes back and fixes things that need to be fixed. Sometimes, fixing them means dismantling them and using them in another piece.

He never really knows what a finished piece will look like. "It never looks the way I imagined, and, man, that makes it really interesting. It is a magical alchemical process. Though the process can be difficult and frustrating, it is a wonderful thing when a piece is finished and you weren't expecting it to be." Michael is usually satisfied with his work, but not for long. He always hopes that his next piece will be better.

What does Michael collect for his artwork? Junk and liquid nails. "Is there really anything else worth mentioning? Oh, some paint too." The junk includes "everything and anything," which he finds in alleys, salvage yards, and secondhand stores. "The world is filled with junk. My philosophy is that we might as well put it to some good use. It is a great metaphor for rebirth." Frequently, freebies also arrive from friends and neighbors.

For his personal pleasure, Michael collects Mexican Dia de los Muertos toys and shrines. "I go calavera crazy every time I go to Mexico for the Day of the Dead. I just can't get enough of those skeletons."

Michael de Meng
Untitled Pez-Dispensing Totem, 2005
6 x 2 x 1 inches (15.2 x 5.1 x 2.5 cm)
Mixed media, found objects
Photo © artist

Chris Giffin
Untitled Sculpture, 2005
32 x 27 x 8 inches (81.3 x 68.6 x 20.3 cm)
Wood hat mold, antique wood and steel wheel, wood mold, metal letters and numbers, cut tin, screwed hat to mold, bird nest, steel wire, feathers, tin crown, fishing lure, antique doll eyes, wood game pieces, nuts, bolts
Photo © Ron Sawyer

CHRIS GIFFIN COMES FROM THE Pacific Northwest, land of sea and mountains galore, and says that nature plays a big part in what inspires her. "There is something about a beautifully shaped branch or a bird's nest that is so simple yet says so much." She uses organic materials in her work in order to perfect a message or just purvey beauty.

Both Chris's mother and father were creative artists, and she thinks of them as her greatest inspirations. Her father actually had a product line that he created from recycled materials and sold to department stores in the late 1940s. It's no wonder that Chris says art was a large part of what kept her hands busy when she was a child.

Chris's formal training is in ceramics; she was a ceramist for 12 years, during which time she created sculptural art. As far as her recycled/found object/altered art goes, she's almost entirely self-taught. She did glean experience as a designer for a company that made a production line of hand-crafted functional home products and jewelry, especially with the engineering of a design into the production phase. After that job, Chris felt comfortable designing and producing her own one-of-a-kind pieces, and marketing them through art fairs, galleries, and exhibitions. She's been doing this work for 15 years now and is in love with it.

Chris has always worked in several mediums. "The commonality [among] them all is that I always approach each with a sense of spontaneity, which gives each piece uniqueness."

Leonardo da Vinci in one of Chris's favorite artists; she really appreciates his imagination, his capacity to think outside the box, and his apparent refusal to set any limitations on his creativeness. "He was all over the place. I particularly admire his inventions. Everything he did was magnificent."

Among the living artists she admires are Kiff Slemmons (for her wit, wisdom, and humor); Keith Lo Bue (for his small works of wonder—magical and mysterious); and Thomas Mann, whose wall boxes and statement-oriented, one-of-a-kind jewelry Chris finds dynamic and beautifully designed.

Chris's inspirations come from a variety of sources. Sometimes she creates a piece with an idea in mind, depending on the disposition of a gallery showing. But her inspiration can also come directly from a found object. "I will find objects that just get me pumped, and produce a series of art pieces incorporating those objects." Her main sources of inspiration, however, are the materials that she has on hand.

Her ideas for a piece are often developed from what Chris describes as "playtime" in her studio. "I feel chronically inspired and go into my studio and play. It's a spontaneous vision, as I have no idea what I will come up with. Once I start playing, though, and a design has been established, I finish it immediately." Chris says that as she works, she fiddles and jumps. "I pull things together from a vast array of visual stimuli, and if I know my methods,

Chris Giffin
Left, *For Now Clock*, 2004; right, *Untitled Sculpture*, 2004
Left, 16 x 6 x 5½ inches (40.6 x 15.2 x 14 cm); right, 12¾ x 12 x 15¼ inches (32.2 x 30.5 x 38.5 cm)
Left, steel meat grinder case, erector set parts, glass dome, antique dial, tobacco tin, anagrams, steel cone, wood block, brass tag, nuts, bolts; right, wood duck decoy, hand cut tins for wings, steel spacer, steel wire bulb cover, metal fishing lure, antique doll eyes, wood game pieces, vinyl disks, rubber toy wheels, steel rods, nuts, bolts, nails
Photo © Ron Sawyer

Chris Giffin
Doll Decoy Structure, 2004
12½ x 6¾ x 15 inches (31.8 x 17.1 x 38.1 cm)
Wood duck decoy, metal doll head, composite doll arms, tintype, brass tag, wood mold, metal tag, vinyl disks nailed in, antique metal wheels, wire, nuts and bolts
Photo © Ron Sawyer

[a piece] can come together quickly through the work process." But experimentation is also important to Chris. She says she has to "fiddle around with what is actually practical and will work with a new method or idea."

Cold connection—a process she loves—has been her working technique for the last 15 years. "It's so diverse. All of my work is screwed together with nuts and bolts, and it really satisfies what I am trying to accomplish. I can layer and have depth. None of my work is really two-dimensional. I think I lean towards the sculptural. I produce functional, wearable, and sculptural items, and they are all objects that have three-dimensional qualities."

When Chris starts a piece, she has only the vaguest picture in her mind of what it might look like. And, she explains, because most of what she does is really a spontaneous process, she usually feels very pleased when the work comes out the way it does. "Its transformation is almost a surprise to me… It's like a weird blessing.

Chris collects everything and anything that she loves. Her only criteria are that her collected objects be vintage or antique; she covets things from the 19th century up to the 1940s. "These objects don't lie," she says. "Their patinas tell the story." In her studio she amasses any number of different objects, including anything old or rusty. "I have piles of rusty old machine parts to play with. I love that stuff."

Like many other artists these days, she has to search far and wide in order to come up with appropriate "junk." She travels widely, so she's able to scour entire regions of the country, where she searches at flea markets, antique fairs, swap meets, surplus yards, recycling centers, second-hand stores, and antique malls. "Has anybody heard of eBay? That's where everything has gone. I still love the hunt. It's so physical and visceral."

Working with found objects appeals to Chris precisely because she's a collector who loves junk and because she believes in recycling as a lifestyle. "It's the perfect venue for my artistic expression. What am I going to do with all this stuff if I don't turn it over?" Fortunately, her practical nature balances her obsessiveness.

As well as the objects themselves, Chris loves the tactile element of her work and the "ability to force [her] will to control these objects and transform them into pieces of art." Chris paints, too, and plans to combine the two mediums in her future work. "But my philosophy stays the same: spontaneous creative combustion and the surprise at completion. Ahh, the mystery of the mind."

She uses organic materials in her work in order to perfect a message or just purvey beauty.

Altered Objects

Throughout this book, I hope you've found a wealth of inspiration and information. The featured projects in this section include instructions that explain the general process that the artist used to create that particular piece. Although you're probably familiar with many if not all of these processes, the artists have used them in different and innovative ways. Perhaps you've used solvent transfers to transfer imagery to paper. Have you ever used them on fabric or on a large-scale piece (see page 117)? Have you worked with collage? How about using a single image serially in different variations and forms (see page 104)? Perhaps your eyes will be opened to working with natural objects in a fresh way (see page 123).

Each one of these projects has something different to teach you about working with an object. Should you avoid using a turtle shell in your work? Of course not. What you choose to do with a shell might not be the same as what Sarah Urquhart chose to do. How could it? Sarah's unique responses to her shell dictated what she did with it. I would never have seen the shell in the same way as she did. Neither would you.

Each of us as an artist brings something special—something

unique—to an object we're working with. This book encourages you to discover your own way to alter objects—ways that only you can imagine, envision, and create.

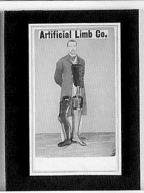

les hommes

CREATED BY TERRY TAYLOR

Speaking for myself, inspiration rarely takes wing immediately. But when it does, it's a real pleasure to be carried away on a rampage of creative fury. This multipart project—three in one—is an example of what can happen when you allow yourself to follow your creative muse from one point to another and another.

materials

Vintage *carte de visite*

Milagros

Found objects

Miniature frames

Foam-core board

Clear plastic sheeting

Brass escutcheon pins

Brass tubing

Vintage objects, imagery, and text

Loteria card

Decorative papers

process

L'Homme Encadré (The Framed Man)

1 A *carte de visite* of this solitary gentleman sat unused in my workspace for more than a year and a half. The chance juxtaposition of a simple milagro with the photograph (I was working on another piece when it happened) sent me on a creative exploration I wasn't expecting—and then on to the creation of two other pieces.

2 When I placed the milagro of the arm on the photograph, I immediately thought to look for a matching leg in my boxes of tiny bits and pieces. While poking around for a leg, I found the top-hat game piece. I liked the way both the milagros and the top hat worked with the image, but I wasn't satisfied with simply gluing them to the image.

3 The idea of framing the image appealed to me. I looked through my stash of frames and rediscovered a couple of square, miniature frames I had forgotten. When I placed one frame on the image, I was intrigued with how the image looked cut in half. Since I had two frames, I thought, why not split the image in half? This presented a problem that I needed to solve. I could hang the two framed halves separately, but keeping the two halves connected visually, if not physically, was more to my liking.

4 I made several full-sized photocopies of the image, adjusting the color tone somewhat to enhance the sepia quality of the original. This was the first of many, many trips to the copy shop.

Next, I made a cardboard template to fit in the frame, then used the template to mark the upper and lower portions of the image. After the portions were cut out, I mounted them on foam-core board and trimmed them to fit snugly inside the frames.

I used the template to mark the clear plastic sheeting and then cut out each square.

5 Simply gluing the milagros to the clear plastic sheeting was an easy option but not one I wanted to use. Instead, I decided to mimic the look of rivets or nails to hold the milagros in place. I marked the position of each milagro and drilled through the plastic sheeting.

I chose brass escutcheon pins rather than common nails. Their color mimicked the gold on the frames. I cut one pin with wire cutters, dabbed a bit of glue on the end of the pin, and then pushed the pin through the plastic sheeting and into the foam-core board, anchoring the milagro in place on the image.

I drilled small holes in the top hat as well as the frame and nailed the hat into place.

6 Using brass tubing to create columns between the two frames appealed to me visually. I made marks for six holes on the bottom of one frame and the top of another. Using a drill bit slightly smaller in diameter than the tubing, I drilled the marked holes.

Next, I cut six short lengths of brass tubing and inserted them in the holes to join the two frames.

The images were inserted into the frames and secured in place with artist's tape.

Such a handsome gentleman. I was drawn to his elegant white breeches (one dare not refer to them as pants), the natty cutaway coat, and the empty, nondescript space he stands in. Anonymous images such as this are rich sources of inspiration and potential canvases for flights of creative fancy.

Terry Taylor

Même Plus d'Hommes (Even More Men)

1 I used the image to create a birthday token for a friend—adding a vintage pin and a bit of text. But once I finished that piece, I didn't want to stop. Literally. When I was asked to participate in a gallery exhibit for Father's Day, I immediately hit on the idea of creating one large piece using the image. But not a single large image: I set myself the task of creating 100 small pieces to be exhibited in a grid at one time.

2 The image was photocopied and mirrored for visual interest. Then I gathered materials to collage on the image. My collection of dictionaries provided many of the images, as did a vintage mail-order catalog. Once I started using those images, other sources of imagery presented themselves: rubber stamps, image transfers, stencils, and imagery from contemporary sources. The image was obscured or multiplied; the background was replaced or adorned.

3 As I worked, small objects began to make their way onto the collaged images. Buttons, beads, mica, and more were added

to some of them. In one, a moon-faced, glass cufflink echoed the lunar loteria card.

4 Then text, as well, became an important aspect of the pieces. Puns, definitions, and scraps of poetry were all fodder for the creative process. Corduroy, after all, is the cloth of kings. I resisted placing a crown on this piece, but not on others.

Homme Avec Un Point de Vue
(Man with a Point of View)

1 On one of the small collages, I glued an image of an old-fashioned stereoscope; it made the gentleman look otherworldly—an alien from another planet. I liked it. I wasn't sure why, but something about it was appealing to me. As I worked on other images, I kept looking at this alien creature I had created,

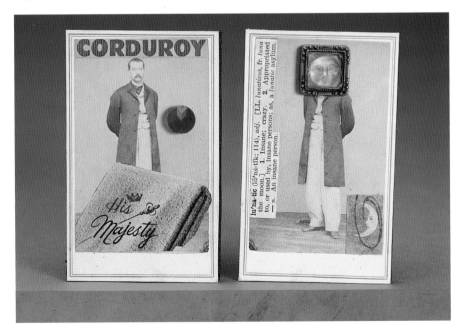

trying to figure out why I was so fascinated with this particular image.

One day of the blue, I remembered that one of my very favorite objects as a child was a stereoscope that belonged to my grandfather. I'd forgotten that the stereoscope was mine and tucked away under the bed. Did I rush to find it? You bet I did. I decided that I would play with my otherworldly gentleman and make cards for my stereoscope.

2 I photocopied the collaged image and enlarged it; I mirrored and duplicated the image in other sizes as well. Imagery and text were added to the photocopies before they were mounted on mat board for strength.

3 I decided that I would try my hand at creating a card for the stereoscope. Using two mirrored images and some lettering, I fashioned a card that actually worked! The images and the letters—L and O on one image, O and K on the other—merge to spell out the prime directive for all of us.

north/south/east/west
(my nest at home is best)

CREATED BY LK LUDWIG

A confection of the imagination,

Pure fancy, and delight.

Oh, to be the bird darting home to such a sight!

materials

Wooden cigar box

Single-bulb candle lamp

Spray paint

Vintage imagery and text

Clear acrylic sealer

Transparency film

Natural elements: twigs, bird's
nest, leaves, and eggs

Miniature wood fencing

Wire mesh

Spray adhesive

Patina solution

Clear acrylic sealer

Mica

Brass lamp trim

Dollhouse door

Found objects

process

1 LK used a cigar box to create the basic form of the house. She removed the lid and one of the short sides. A part of the lid was fashioned into the peaked roof. A hole was cut into the back of the assembled house so that a small candle lamp could fit inside.

2 Multiple light coats of spray paint were used to give the house form a base coating. LK drilled a hole in the back of the house. She enlarged the hole as needed to accommodate a single-bulb candle lamp.

3 Paper photocopies of vintage imagery and text were collaged onto the sides and roof of the house. The bird images amplify the theme of home and nest. When the collage was dry, LK gave it a light coat of clear acrylic sealer.

In addition, while LK was making her paper color photocopies, one bird image was copied onto a transparency. She envisioned using it later on when she added the dollhouse door to the house.

4 LK collaged the back wall of the house form, then arranged the interior assemblage of graceful, tiny twigs and miniature fencing, working from back to front. She used a heavy-duty glue to anchor the objects.

How-to Tip

If you plan to enclose a box form permanently, be sure you use the heaviest-duty (and most reliable) glue you can find to secure any objects inside. Once those objects are enclosed, getting to them to make any repairs is nearly impossible. Alternatively, design a way to get inside the box if necessary. Many of Joseph Cornell's boxes are constructed with backs that may be removed if objects break or need arranging.

5 A scrim of wire mesh was cut to match the shape of the house. LK embellished the mesh with subtle silhouettes of leaf shapes.

Leaves were coated with spray adhesive and then adhered to the screen. LK filled a spray bottle with a commercial patina solution and then sprayed the mesh. After the patina solution changed the surface of the mesh, the leaves were removed, and the mesh was rinsed with water. To preserve the patina, LK gave the mesh a light coat of clear acrylic sealer.

LK used heavy-duty glue to attach the dried scrim to the house. Next, she cut strips of brass lamp trim to outline the shape and glued them in place on top of the screen.

6 LK removed the center panel on the dollhouse door. She trimmed the transparency with the bird image and fitted it on the back surface of the door. Then she glued the entire door assembly to the front of the house.

7 To echo the twigs inside, LK added wired floral branches—trimmed with faux pearls, beads, and tiny bells—to the outside of the box.

8 The completed house is imbued with a mysterious but welcoming glow created by placing the candle lamp into the hole that LK created in the first step.

House and home—my little nests in the wide world—are the sources of inspiration for this piece. I love working with the imagery surrounding houses. Birds and the metaphor of nest as home occur frequently in my work; they're natural offshoots of my life as a single mom. Natural elements and the natural world provide imagery and inform my palette.

LK Ludwig

silly men

CREATED BY LOU MCCULLOCH

This multilayered piece, with doors that open onto surprise after surprise, is elegantly amusing.

materials

Book

Scrap wood

Mica

Hand-colored picture

Cigar box

Small screws

Wooden type blocks

Acrylic paint

Small tin boxes

Vintage text and imagery

Wood block

Found objects: funnel, compass, game pieces, calipers, and metal star shape

Brass straps

Miniature papier-mâché boxes

Chipboard letters

Vintage tintype

Decorative papers

Fibers

process

1 Lou gathered together a diverse variety of materials to play with. Using a cigar box for the torso was a natural choice, as was using the large letters as a base for the piece. Can you imagine fiddling around with a compass and calipers until an "aha" moment occurs when the two objects form a basic stick figure (see next page)?

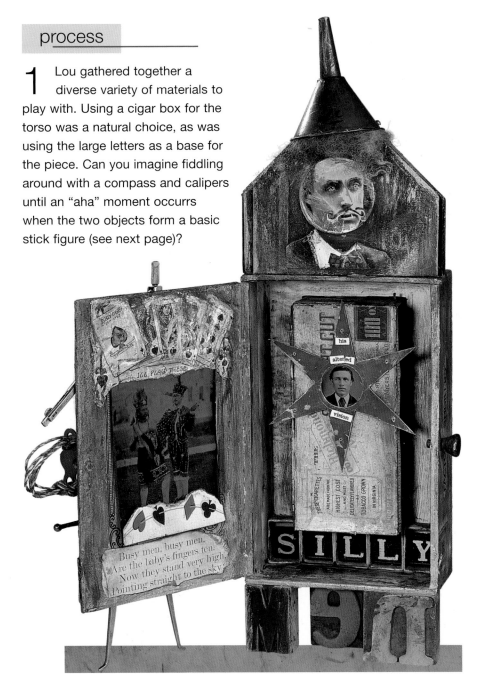

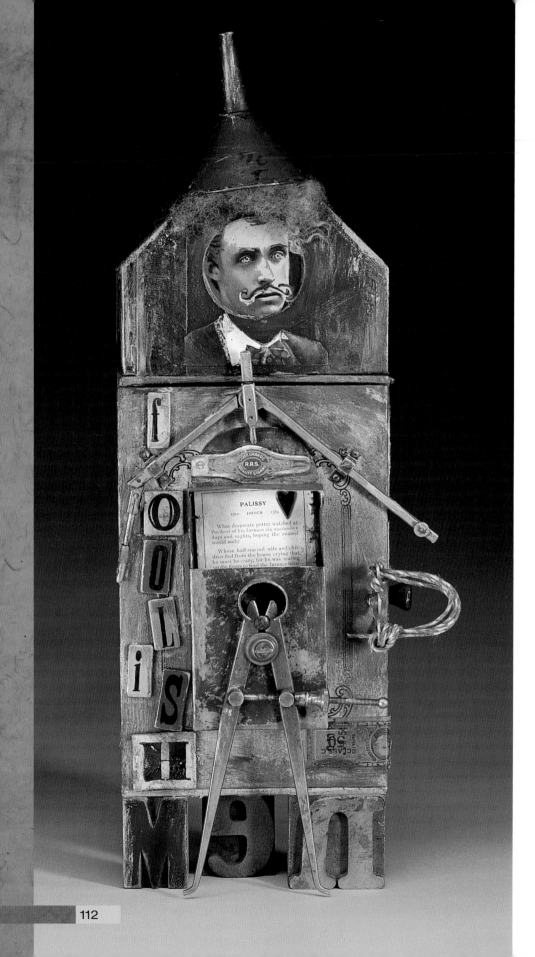

2 To create the head portion of the figure, Lou cut a book into a triangular shape. To support the cut book, she cut the same shape out of a piece of wood.

Lou cut a circular opening in the book's cover, backed the opening with mica, and slipped a hand-colored picture behind the mica. Then she glued the book and wood shape together before attaching them to the top of the box with small screws. The wooden letter type blocks were also attached to the cigar box with screws.

3 Disparate parts can be made less jarring by giving them light washes of color. Lou used washes of blue acrylic paint—dictated by the blue letter m—to tie together the head and torso. Using the same color palette, Lou tinted the interior of the box as well.

How-to Tip

If you've applied acrylic medium to a box with a door or lid, don't store the piece with the door or lid closed. Even if you think the coat of medium is dry, it's best to slip a small piece of waxed paper between the two surfaces to prevent them from sticking together.

4 Lou cut away a portion of the lid on one of the small boxes. Vintage text was collaged to the interior of the box. The brilliant choice of text—a biography of the mad French potter Palissy, whose phantasmagoric ceramics were thought silly by many—fits the theme of the piece. Then Lou secured the box to the front panel of the cigar box. Thinking ahead to the next step in the process, Lou slipped a block of wood into the box.

The calipers were secured to the wood in the metal box with a screw and washer. Lou created small brass straps to hold the compass, and then used small screws to attach it to the box lid.

5 Lou added color to a second small box and then collaged elements to it. A tintype and a metal star were bold choices for the outside; an assortment of vintage imagery was adhered to the interior.

Small papier-mâché boxes were given washes of blue acrylic before Lou added a letter to each: S-i-l-l-y. These elements were added to the interior as well.

6 The inspirational tintype was adhered to the back of the cigar box lid. Various decorative papers and text were judiciously

applied for decorative as well as practical reasons. The card imagery above the tintype hides the ends of the screws that were used to attach the compass. Yes, necessity is also the mother of improvisation.

7 As final touches, Lou added a small knob to the side of the cigar box and a key to the lid. The key, with the addition of fibers, functions as a handle to make it easier to open the box. No doubt there was one crowning glory "aha" moment in the entire process when the funnel became a hat.

A large antique tintype with two men wearing costumes and funny hats was the initial inspiration for this piece. The men made me think of the word "silly," and I knew I had wooden type letters to spell "men." I used blue accents on the piece, simply because the letter M was already painted blue.

Lou McCulloch

santo desconocido
(unknown saint)

CREATED BY TERRY TAYLOR

This piece is a good example of my ruminative working methods.
The inspiration for the piece came first, the execution much later.

materials

Vintage imagery

Canvas cot

Stencil

Acrylic paint

Ink

Vintage paper tag

process

1 The image of the bandaged figure came from a vintage, pocket-sized Army medical manual. I was attracted to the figure's stylized raiment of bandages and its open-palmed, welcoming stance. It reminded me of saintly images on icons and other religious paintings—figures whose forms were appealing, but whose actions were unclear, or whose stories were unknown to me. I knew I wanted to use the image in a piece, but didn't know precisely how. I kept tabs on the image for a long time, and would look at it every so often, hoping it would spark an idea.

2 At one point, while I was looking at the image, I remembered an old army cot from my childhood. My brother and I would beg to play with this cot, and occasionally our parents would set it up for us. The combination of the bandaged figure and the cot was irresistible. I simply had to locate that cot. But it was nowhere to be found.

A couple of years—literally—went by. Then one, sunny summer day at the local flea market, I spied a

For many years, much of my artwork has been inspired and informed by my interest in religious icons of various faiths. Their simple, mysterious beauty inspires me, especially when the objects are evidently created by untrained craftsmen and are tenderly cared for by their owners.

I strive to create pieces that don't look like parodies, but take on a quiet life of their own. Sometimes they work; other times they don't. In retrospect, the best pieces work because I do very little to the original objects that inspired them. Stains, scratches, and coats of paint are left intact. Adding something of interest or curiosity to the inherent beauty of a found object satisfies my quest to change the meaning and function of the original object.

Terry Taylor

bundle of canvas and wood on the ground. I knew exactly what it was, asked to examine the canvas cover, and didn't even think of bargaining.

3 I asked a friend to scan the image and scale the size to fit the cot's dimensions as closely as possible. He tiled the image onto several sheets and printed it out.

I photocopied the scans and used a solvent transfer method to transfer the image onto the canvas surface (see page 14). Then I covered the transferred image with a cloth and heat-set the image using a hot iron.

4 A small flame motif was stenciled onto the exposed chest with acrylic paint. I added a circular nimbus around the head, using gold paint and ink. I stenciled the words "*santo desconocido*" onto a vintage paper tag and attached it to the cot.

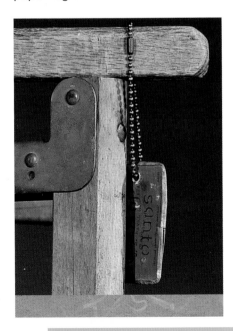

Santo Desconocido
31 x 77 x 18 inches (78.7 x 195.5 x 45.7 cm)
McConville Collection
Photo by Steve Mann

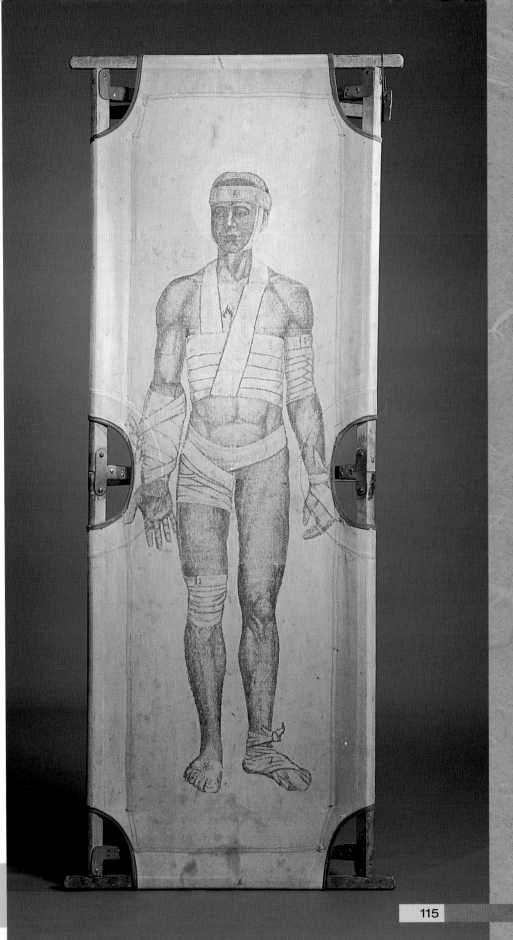

ties that bind

CREATED BY LINA TRUDEAU OLSON

Personal, heartfelt, and mysterious, this piece welcomes a different interpretation from each viewer.

materials

Scissors

Text papers

Wooden box

Cardboard box

Dress-pattern pages

Acrylic paint

Jute cording

Wooden tiles and disks

Buttons

Decorative papers

Dress patterns

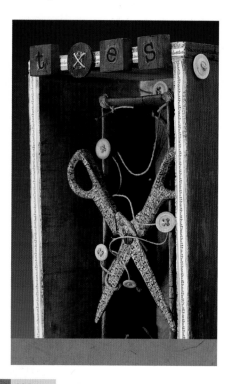

process

1 The genesis of this piece began with the scissors. Lina wanted to cover the object with text. She used different typefaces for the text, photocopying and reducing a single word: "family." She made "tons of tiny photocopies" to collage onto the scissors.

Lina found collaging over the scissors "quite therapeutic and time-consuming." Completing this simple, repetitive task became meditative. She admitted that it would have been a lot less time-consuming to use a computer to compose a sheet of text, but she liked the simple act of cutting out each word individually.

2 Lina wanted to suspend the scissors inside the wooden box. She used a smaller cardboard box to form a support for them. The cardboard box was collaged with dress-pattern pages that had been colored with a wash of acrylic paint. Then the corners of the box were strengthened with a wrapping of jute cording.

3 The exterior box was distressed by layering multiple coats of acrylic paint. Between coats of paint, Lina abraded the surface with coarse sandpaper.

4 Lina affixed the smaller box inside the larger one with a heavy-duty adhesive. Then she adhered the scissors to the box, again with a heavy-duty adhesive.

5 Decorative details—more jute cording, buttons, wooden disks, and tiles—were added. Letters were collaged to both the tiles and discs before they were glued to the box. Jute and buttons were intertwined between the scissor blades and handles, and then attached to the outside of the cardboard box.

The proverbial "apron strings" and their being "cut" at one point or another were the inspirations for this piece. It attempts to address both the positive and negative ways in which our families are bound and the nature of the relationships secured by these ties that bind us. For me, this piece illustrates the tenuous balance between support and restraint that exists in my family. As the work evolved, so did my perception of my relationship with my family. It's a complex thing: Who is responsible for the "cutting" and who wields the "scissors"?

Lina Trudeau Olson

tableau trio

CREATED BY LOU MCCULLOCH

The imagination of childhood is celebrated in this trio of assemblages—valve-handle wheels for the cart, and a shoe tree for a stroller.

materials

- Wooden shoe tree stretcher
- Vintage photographs
- Thin plywood
- Wood bases
- Vintage rag doll
- Found objects—valve handles, doll
- Scrap wood
- Nails
- Small screws
- Wood type blocks

process

1 Lou's compositions usually start with one found object: a vintage doll, metal object, or wooden form. For instance, when she found the wooden shoe tree stretcher, the long metal arm immediately made

her think of a handle, and the wood form of something to push—a stroller, perhaps, or a wagon.

2 Once Lou chooses an image from her collection of vintage photographs, she photocopies and enlarges it to match the scale of one of the found objects she has chosen. Then each image is hand-colored with oil crayons and inks. Lou mounts each image onto thin plywood and then cuts out the image with a jigsaw.

A sitting image of a child was the perfect choice for the shoe stretcher. All Lou had to do was add two vintage wheels to turn it into a stroller.

3 Originally, Lou had envisioned someone pushing the stroller, so she needed an image of someone standing to complete the composition. The perfect image in her collection of photographs was a woman, but she was dressed in an old-fashioned, jersey bathing suit.

It's always interesting to see what happens when a piece changes direction while you work on it. Unless you're willing to put the piece aside until you find just the right thing, go with the flow. Let one thing lead naturally to another. If the woman was wearing a bathing suit, the tableau would take a seaside detour. So Lou used her saw to cut out wave forms from a piece of wood.

What if you could cap-
ture a moment in time?
Or preserve a three-
dimensional snapshot
that gave you a glimpse
into the past? These
tableaus are composed
with found objects and
reproductions of the
antique photographs
which have beguiled me
all of my life. My compo-
sitions usually start with
a single found object—a
doll, a toy, or a form—
which I combine with a
vintage image that
appeals to me.

Lou McCulloch

4 When Lou is inspired by her images, finding the right object sometimes becomes frustrat-ing. A carte de visite picturing a small boy with a toy sailboat sent her on a search for a toy sailboat. Unfortunately, the toy sailboats she found were either too expensive or had been sold when she went back to get them. The vintage rag doll she had purchased previously need-ed a wagon to ride in.

Lou solved both of those problems by fashioning the objects herself. Nails and small pieces of wood are all that she needed to create the toy boat and the wagon. An inspired use of found objects—in this case, cast-metal valve handles—resulted in the wheels for the wagon.

5 Lou insists that her greatest find at any flea market was a type tray filled with wooden letters. It's obvious that she's used them in a signature way in her work. She delights in mixing the variety of fonts and sizes in her stash. And she's not bothered by the fact that some of the letters have to be used in their reversed forms.

6 The trio of tableaus is mounted on simple wooden bases that were stained to match the patina of the letters. Lou finds that small screws are best for attaching the mounted images, the type blocks, and other objects to each base.

How-to Tip

If you see something that speaks to you or that sets your creative juices flow-ing, buy it then and there if you can afford it (or can rationalize the purchase to yourself). It won't be there when you come back to buy it. And you'll regret the missed opportunity each and every time.

the gypsy's cart

CREATED BY SARAH URQUHART

The individual eye creatively transforms a found object in totally unexpected ways. It's hard to imagine that any two artists would alter this carapace with the same results.

materials

Onionskin paper

Acrylic medium

Turtle shell

Wood

Metal jar lid

Acrylic paints

Wood strip

Metal rod

Tissue paper

Felt

Copper sheet

Mica

Miniature hinge

Ring box

Glass-topped tin

Glass vials

Found objects—metal ammonite,
thin chain, vintage metal toy
wheel, ring box, miniature dice

Vintage imagery

Copper eyelets

process

1 Sarah drew what appears to be abstract imagery on a sheet of onionskin paper. In fact, the drawing is composed of Sarah's interpretations of aerial views of all the places she has lived: the west coast of the United States; Poitiers, France; Butterset, England; and her present home in Swannanoa, North Carolina. The linear quality of her drawing of winding streets and grids of towns complements the divided segments of the turtle shell. She cut out the maps and glued them to the shell with gel medium.

2 Carefully noting the lips of the bottom of the shell, Sarah decided that rather than attaching something to the shell permanently, she would use the lips as a guide. They would enable her to slip the turtle shell on and off. Sarah cut a thin piece of wood to fit inside the shell. The cart slips in and out amazingly well; it's an inspired bit of imaginative engineering.

3 In her stash, Sarah had one metal wheel from an old tin toy that she wanted to use on her cart. Needing a second wheel, Sarah found a similarly sized metal jar lid and painted it with acrylics to complement—not copy precisely—the vintage wheel. The compass-points design on the wheel echoes the many points of Sarah's journeys.

Next, Sarah fashioned an axle base using a small strip of wood. She wired a small metal rod to the wood, and then attached the wood to the wooden base of the cart.

4 Patterned tissue paper was applied to the wooden cart base with acrylic medium. A single layer of felt tops off the cart base.

5 Sarah fashioned a door for the cart out of copper sheet. She cut irregular shapes out of the copper to echo the shapes on the shell. Small mica shapes were cut out to be placed on top of the copper. Both types of shape were riveted together to form the door.

Sarah drilled tiny holes in the shell. Next, she wired a tiny hinge to the door, and then wired the door to the hinge.

6 A small ring box, tin, and vials were glued to the cart base. A metal ammonite nailed to the base created a handle to which Sarah attached a thin chain with which to pull the cart.

I found this turtle shell already bleached by the sun. For some unknown reason, its shape—who knows why?—reminded me of a gypsy caravan's arched roof. I began to think about all the places I have lived and how, like a gypsy, I have carried little bits and pieces from all of those places with me as I moved from place to place. All of the objects in the interior—the tiny heart and the vials—represent those bits and pieces.

Sarah Urquhart

icarian folly

CREATED BY TERRY TAYLOR

It would have been easy to glue wings to the figure, but the effect I was after wasn't light or airy. Rueful, bittersweet, and poignant are best expressed with a single broken wing.

materials

Vintage imagery

Iron-on transfer paper

Muslin

Embroidery hoop

China wing

Found chain

Wire

Game letters

Brass tubing

Beeswax

How-to Tip

If you manage to add too much beeswax to a surface, it's easy to remove it. Place one or two layers of absorbent paper on the surface (paper towels or brown paper bags work well). Using a tacking iron or iron, gently heat small areas until you see some staining on the paper. Remove the paper and check the surface. Continue this process until you have achieved the covering you wish.

process

1 I've used other images from the same early 20th-century exercise manual in at least three different pieces. The static poses of the boys and girls are so ritualistic and mysterious once they're removed from their context. This image was photocopied onto an iron-on transfer paper and then applied to muslin before being placed in the embroidery hoop. Once the image was stretched taut in the hoop, it sat for a very, very long time in my studio, waiting to be finished.

2 I considered using this wing fragment in other pieces but didn't like the idea of gluing it onto something—that seemed too easy. Suspending it in the air, on the other hand, appealed to me. However, I didn't want to add anything to the wing that would interfere with its pure, white form.

After much thought, I decided to drill a hole in the wing and thread a chain through it. Drilling through glass or china isn't as tricky as it might seem, but it does take some care. Use a diamond-coated drill bit for the best result.

I'm a methodical, plodding worker; unrelated bits and pieces sit in my studio for years until they coalesce as I think they should. I move things around, placing bits and parts on different pieces just to see what they might look like. When I get in a hurry and try to force a piece into a finished state, the end results invariably don't satisfy me. I prefer to ponder all of my options and variations before I finally assemble a piece. Consequently, pieces sit around in my studio, in various stages of completion, for a long time. Yes, the studio is a mess.

This delicate, broken wing sat on my studio worktable or was stashed away in my box of goodies for longer than I care to admit. I was drawn to both the fragility of the piece and its potent symbolism, but I didn't have a clue what to do with it. However, once I finally decided, the entire piece came together with surprising speed.

Terry Taylor

I chose this handmade chain, which I found at a flea market, because I could cut a link and thread it through the wing without having to solder the link back together again.

3 I drilled a very small hole through the bottom of the embroidery hoop, threaded some wire through the hole, and made a simple wire loop to suspend the chain from.

4 My selection for a title was not meant to be fey or inspirational, but rather to contrast with the broken wing and the frozen movement of the figure. Gluing the flat letter tiles to the curved top of the embroidery hoop wasn't an option: I knew I wouldn't be happy with the finished look and would worry about the letters popping off. Instead, I decided to use handmade tube rivets to attach each letter to the hoop.

Short lengths of brass tubing were cut slightly longer than the height of each letter. Then I drilled holes, slightly smaller than the diameter of the brass tubing, along the top portion of the hoop and through each of the letter tiles.

One end of each tube was flared out with a flaring tool. (An awl or nail will do this job.) Each tube was threaded up from the inside of the hoop, a letter was fitted onto it, and then the top end of the tube was flared out to hold the letter in place.

5 As a final touch, I decided to give the fabric several light coats of beeswax.

Artist Biographies

John Borero considers himself a storyteller, and his found object sculptures have been described as mesmerizing, provocative, captivating, playful, and disturbing...often in the same breath! John's inspiration grows from his deep interest in archeology, anthropology, mythology, and theology. Many of his pieces reveal a strong sense of spirituality and a personal search for the Divine. You can see more of John's work at www.johnborero.com.

Patricia Chapman is an assemblage and collage artist residing in Santa Fe, New Mexico. She utilizes found objects and appropriated imagery to create psychological, social, and political commentaries about life, love, and other impossible situations. More of her art can be viewed at www.thepatstudio.com.

Janet Cooper lives in Sheffield, Massachusetts. Her mixed-media work has sold at various galleries and museum shops in the United States, Europe, and Asia, and exhibited in several museum shows on recycling. Her website is www.janetcooperdesigns.com.

Joe de Camillis grew up in Colorado. He studied creative writing at UCLA before becoming a painter. He exhibits at craft shows and has shown at numerous galleries, most recently at Blue Spiral, in Asheville, North Carolina. He lives in Birmingham, Alabama.

Michael de Meng is an assemblage artist whose work is heavily influenced by Latin American art forms such as retablos, ex votos, and milagros. Born in Southern California, he now works and resides in Missoula, calling it "the cultural Mecca of Montana." He exhibits and teaches throughout the world, promoting the alchemy of transforming trash to treasure, and maintains a website at www.michaeldemeng.com.

Chris Giffin grew up in the Pacific Northwest. She trained formally as a ceramicist but has used mixed media in her work for last 15 years. Her work has been showcased in *Found Object Art* (Schiffer, 2001) *Altered Art* (Lark Books, 2004) and *The Fine Art of the Tin Can* (Lark Books, 1996). She lives in Jefferson, Oregon.

Bobby Hansson, the author of *The Fine Art of the Tin Can* (Lark Books, 1996), has made artwork from tin cans for more than 40 years. His work has been shown at the American Craft Museum, the Renwick Gallery of the Smithsonian American Art Museum, and the Oakland Museum, as well as many galleries and schools. He has taught at numerous institutions, including Haystack Mountain School of Crafts, Parsons School of Design, and Penland School of Crafts. He builds vehicles for kinetic sculpture races, constructs Cubist guitars and horns from every imaginable material, and makes mail art almost too ornate to send. He lives in Rising Sun, Maryland.

Margert Krulijac has been creating since the moment she touched her first crayon. A self-taught artist comfortable with all mediums, she warns that no object is safe from her altering ways! Margert teaches at industry trade shows, as well as several times a month at her local scrapbook store. She designs for two publications, and her work has been featured in many others. She calls southern West Virginia home. Her website is www.mementosdiarte.com.

LK Ludwig is a mixed-media artist living in rural northwest Pennsylvania. Her work may be seen in a variety of magazines and several books, including *Artful Paper Dolls* (Lark Books, 2006). She teaches occasional workshops around the country. LK's website, at gryphonsfeather.typepad.com, is a blog of life, work, art, and family.

Susan McBride is an artist who has worked in the field of graphic design for the last 20 years. She has sketched and painted all of her life. She's the author and illustrator of *The Don't-Get-Caught Doodle Notebook* (Lark Books, 2005), *The I'm-so-Bored-Doodle Notebook* (Lark Books, 2006), and *Office Doodle Notebook* (Lark Books, 2007). She lives in Asheville, North Carolina, with her family, two cats, and a crazy dog.

Lou McColluch works as a senior designer for *Altered Arts* magazine and has authored a book about paper Americana as well as a reference for card photograph collectors. Some of Lou's work can be seen in the magazines *Artitude*, *Altered Arts*, and *Cloth, Paper, Scissors*. She currently builds assemblages with her talented husband, many of which can be seen at alteredlou.blogspot.com, metamorphosis.typepad.com/metamorphosis/, and www.cafepress.com/glimpses

Nicole McConville is an artist with a background in correspondence art and collage. Her assemblage constructions reflect a passion for salvaging found objects and creating a new environment to tell their stories. She has recently shown her work in the United States, England, and Germany. View more of her work at www.sigilation.com.

Eric Allen Montgomery is a Canadian mixed-media sculptor and glass artist living on British Columbia's Sunshine Coast with his tiny black cat Ruby and giant marmalade tabby, Jack The Pumpkin King. He long ago gave up trying to understand his fascination with the world's detritus and only occasionally wishes it would all fit into small tins. His award-winning mixed-media Memory Boxes are available primarily by commission, as well as through selected galleries and exhibitions across North America, and can be seen at www.memoryboxer.ca.

Jean Tomaso Moore is a mixed-media artist who lives and works in Asheville, North Carolina. She has designed projects for numerous Lark books, including *Altered Art* (Lark Books, 2004) and *Artful Paper Dolls* (Lark Books, 2006). Jean can be reached at LeaningTowerArt@msn.com.

Opie and **Linda O'Brien** are mixed-media artists, authors and teachers, who enjoy pushing the envelope in a myriad of ways, using organic, recycled and found materials. They teach art workshops in the United States, Mexico, and Europe. They are the authors of *Metal Craft Discovery Workshop* (North Light, 2005). Their work has also been featured in *Belle Armoire, Art Doll Quarterly, Somerset Studio, Legacy* and the *Craft Report* as well as in art galleries, museum gift shops. They live in Ohio on Lake Erie with their cat Angelus and his cat Angel. For more information about the artists, visit their website at www.burntofferings.com

Lina Trudeau Olson is an elementary art educator in Asheville, North Carolina. She balances her time between the classroom, the studio, and her young family. This lively mix is a constant source of inspiration and enthusiasm. Her work was recently published in *Altered Art* (Lark Books, 2004) and *Artful Paper Dolls* (Lark Books, 2006).

Teresa Petersen is an artist living and working in Detroit. After graduating from Michigan State University in 1990 with a dual degree in biology and art, she worked as both a scientific illustrator and a fine artist. In 1998, she received her MFA from Wayne State University and quickly became interested in collage and assemblage. Her work explores women's place in society, both past and present, and the repetition and idealization of women's roles. Intertwined among these ideas are themes of nature, mass consumption, and re-use, and the exploration of these ideas within modern society. More of Teresa's art can be found on her website at teresapetersen.com.

James Michael Starr's work might be said to emulate the Japanese concept of wabi-sabi, the beauty of things imperfect and incomplete. He is represented in the permanent collection of the Centre de Documentation sur L'art du Collage in Sergines, France, and participated in Assemblage 100, which toured New Zealand in 2004. His work was most recently included in the French book *L'art du Collage à L'aube du Vingt et Unième Siècle (The Art of Collage at the Dawn of the Twenty-First Century)* and can be viewed at his web site, www.jamesmichaelstarr.com. He lives and works in Dallas, Texas.

Jen Swearington has been altering objects ever since she found a handful of playing cards on a Brooklyn street in 1996. She lives in Asheville, North Carolina, where she creates Jennythreads, her line of handmade silk wearables; she also makes mixed-media quilts from old bed sheets. Her website is www.jennythreads.net.

Terry Taylor is the author of *Altered Art* (Lark Books, 2004), *Artful Paper Dolls* (Lark Books, 2006), *Chain Mail Jewelry* (Lark Books, 2006), and half a dozen other titles all published by Lark Books. He's an acquisitions editor at Lark during the day, and a mixed-media artist and jeweler in the evening and early morning hours. He lives with his cats Bitty and Buddy in West Asheville, North Carolina.

Sarah Urquhart was born in Oregon and has lived all over the world as a child. Always a collector of bits and pieces, she worked in museums for years until moving to Asheville, North Carolina. She had made art quilts and artist books, but in assemblage she found a way to merge her love of odd bits, natural objects, and the stories they tell.

Lynne Whipple has been showing mixed-media artwork for the past 15 years. She is a Florida native and self-taught artist, loves shell-fish, and has very low cholesterol. Her work has appeared in *Altered Art* (Lark Books, 2004), *Artful Paper Dolls* (Lark Books, 2006), and many other titles by Lark Books. Her website is www.whippleart.com.

Jane Wynn is a mixed-media artist from Baltimore, Maryland, who exhibits throughout the United States. With a Masters in Fine Art from Towson University, she has taught foundation art classes at colleges and universities in Maryland. She currently teaches a variety of techniques in jewelry design, mixed media, and assemblage art at workshops around the country. She lives in Baltimore, Maryland with Thomas, her husband and fellow artist, as well as her cats. Visit her website: www.wynnstudio.com.

Featured Astists

Index